XML and InDesign

Dorothy J. Hoskins

O'REILLY®

Beijing · Cambridge · Farnham · Köln · Sebastopol · Tokyo

XML and InDesign

by Dorothy J. Hoskins

Published by O'Reilly Media, Inc., 1005 Gravenstein Highway North, Sebastopol, CA 95472.

O'Reilly books may be purchased for educational, business, or sales promotional use. Online editions are also available for most titles (*http://my.safaribooksonline.com*). For more information, contact our corporate/institutional sales department: 800-998-9938 or *corporate@oreilly.com*.

Editor: Simon St. Laurent	**Copyeditor:** Nancy Kotary
Production Editor: Kristen Borg	**Proofreader:** O'Reilly Production Services
	Cover Designer: Randy Comer
	Interior Designer: David Futato
	Illustrator: Rebecca Demarest

January 2013:   First Edition

Revision History for the First Edition:

2013-01-10   First release

See *http://oreilly.com/catalog/errata.csp?isbn=9781449344160* for release details.

ISBN: 978-1-449-34416-0

[LSI]

Table of Contents

Preface. vii

1. **A Brief Foray into Structured Content (a.k.a. XML)**. 1

2. **InDesign XML Publishing: College Catalog Case Study**. 5
   Data-Like Content Example: The Course Description XML   7
      Data Exported as XML   8
      Modeling the Structure for the Import XML   9
   Topical Content: The Handbook XML   9
      Evaluating the Handbook Text for Structure   9
      Modeling the Structure as a Set of Topics   10
      Iteration and Refinement   11
      Net Results: Vast Improvements in Understanding and Speed 12

3. **Importing XML**. 13
   Doing It Adobe's Way: The Placeholder Approach   13
      Modeling the XML You Want   14
      Importing XML into Placeholders   18
      An Aside: The Scary "Map Styles to Tags" Dialog Message   25
   Mingling Non-XML and XML Content in a Text Flow   26
      Exporting XHTML When XML is in Your InDesign File   29
   Doing It Your Way: Using the Options for Your Own Process   31
      Import XML Using Only Merge—No Other Import Settings   31
      Linking to External XML Files   31
      Creating Text Flows for the Imported XML   32
      The Importance of "Document Order" for Imported XML   32
   Understanding InDesign's XML Import Options   34
      Using "Clone Repeating Text Elements"   35
      Importing Only Elements That Match Structure   37
      Avoiding Overwriting Text Labels in the Placeholder Elements 38

     Deleting Nonmatching Structure, Text, and Layout Components   40

    Importing Images   41

     Inline Image Imports   42

4. Tagging XML in InDesign... **43**

    The Case for Tagging Content: Why You Need XML   43

    Tagging for Import   44

    Tagging for Iterative XML Development   44

     Working Without an Initial DTD   45

5. Looking Forward: InDesign as an XML "Skin"................................ **47**

6. Exporting XML... **49**

    Marking Up (Tagging) Existing Content for XML Export   49

    The Special Case of InDesign Tables (Namespaced XML)   49

     Examining the Table   50

    Tagging Images as XML in InDesign   54

     Image Options in the Export XML Dialog   55

7. Exporting ePub Content (InDesign CS5.5 and CS6)........................... **57**

    Export in XML Order Compared with Page Layout and Article Pane Order   57

    Alternate Layouts and XML Are Not Compatible Features   58

     Untested: Liquid Layout and InDesign Files Containing XML Structure   59

8. Validating XML in InDesign... **61**

    Why Validate?   61

    How to Validate XML in InDesign   61

     Loading a DTD and Getting the Correct Root Element   63

    Authoring with a DTD   63

     Dealing with Validation Problems   64

     Occurrence and Sequences of Elements   67

     Validating Outside of InDesign   68

     Duplicating Structure to Build XML   69

     Cleaning Up Imported XML Content   70

    Fast and Light Credo: Develop Now, Validate Later   70

     Iterating the Information Structure and DTD   70

9. What InDesign Cannot Do (or Do Well) with XML........................... **73**

    The 1:1 Import Conundrum   73

    Bad Characters   74

    Inscrutable Errors, Messages, and Crashes   74

InDesign Is Not an XML Authoring Tool   75

10. **Advanced Topics: Transforming XML with XSL.** **77**
    XSLT for Wrangling XML versus XML Scripting for Automating XML
        Publishing   78
    XSL: Extracting Elements from a Source XML File for a New Use   79
    XSL: Getting the Elements to Sort Themselves   81
    XSL: Getting Rid of Elements You Don't Want   82
    Creating Wrappers for Repeating Chunks   84
    Making a Table from Element Structures   87
    Upcasting Versus Downcasting   90
    Upcasting from HTML to XML for InDesign Import   94
    Downcasting to HTML   94
    Generate a Link with XSLT (Not Automated)   100
    Adding Useful Attributes to XML   101
        A General Formula for Adding Attributes   102
        Generating an id Attribute for a div   102
        Use of the lang Attribute for Translations   103
        Creating an Image href Attribute   103
    A Word about Using Find/Change for XML Markup in InDesign   104

11. **Content Model Depth Issues and Their Impact on Round-Tripping XML.** **107**
    The Challenge of Mapping Deep DTDs to Shallow InDesign Structures   107
    The Challenge of Mapping Shallow Structures to Deep DTD Structures   108
    Use of Semantic ids and Style Names (Expert-Level Development)   109

12. **Brief Notes.** **115**
    A Brief Note about InCopy and XML   115
    A Brief Note about IDML and ICML   117
        Automating InDesign: The Power of IDML and ICML Programming   120
    Summary   128

A. **Resources.** **131**

Preface

From Adobe InDesign CS2 to InDesign CS6, the ability to work with XML content has been built into every version of InDesign. Some of the useful applications are importing database content into InDesign to create catalog pages, exporting XML that will be useful for subsequent publishing processes, and building chunks of content that can be reused in multiple publications. XML is used widely with digital-first publishing workflows.

In this book, we'll play with the contents of a college course catalog and you'll learn how you can use XML for course descriptions, tables, and other content. Underlying principles of XML structure, DTDs, and the InDesign namespace will help you develop your own XML processes. I'll touch briefly on using InDesign to "skin" XML content, exporting as XHTML, InCopy, and the IDML package. Chapter 10, *Advanced Topics: Transforming XML with XSL* includes tips on using XSLT to manipulate XML in conjunction with InDesign.

In this book, I refer to InDesign CS6, and previous versions of the program back to CS3, generically as "InDesign CS." When there are important differences in one version's XML features, I indicate for which version the screenshot or other information applies. Many features remain the same from one version to another. Generally, the screenshots are taken from InDesign CS6 for new content and CS5 for older content. I assume that you already know quite a bit about InDesign typographic styles and layout features because you want to use InDesign to do something with XML. In particular, I assume that you understand the role that paragraph and character styles play in consistent typography throughout an InDesign document or set of documents in the same InDesign template. (If you are new to these concepts, please refer to Adobe's InDesign CS built-in Help→Styles or Peachpit Press's *Real World Adobe InDesign CS6*.)

The power that XML brings to the InDesign world is summed up in the word *interoperability*, which means that the same content in XML format can be used in multiple applications or processes—and not solely inside InDesign. XML is typically used for creating HTML for websites, but it can also be used to create rich text, PDF, or plain text files. XML does not inherently have "presentation styles": the appearance of an XML file depends upon the way in which it is formatted and used by applications. The main purpose of XML is to provide a reliable structure of content so that it can be processed consistently once an application has rules for presenting the structure visually. (For more information on XML, see O'Reilly's *XML in a Nutshell*, 3rd ed.)

For example, in a course catalog, there might be information that resides in a database in a set of tables (course descriptions, programs of study, faculty and staff directory, etc.). The information in the tables is the "content"; the way that it is organized in table columns, rows, and cells is its "structure." If we save the data as XML, it becomes the structured content that we need, but now it is no longer bound to the database application. It's ready to use and reuse in other applications, including InDesign CS6.

 InDesign has features for importing and working with data in comma-separated-values (*.csv*) or tab-delimited (*.txt*) text format. But XML provides for a much more complex information structure to be imported into InDesign.

We'll look at how and why you might want to tag content as XML in InDesign and export it to use in other applications. A theoretical workflow for XML with XSLT to create web page output will give you ideas for what you might want to do with your own InDesign documents.

XML publishing has traditionally been a process of generating PDF or HTML files from XML sources. These generated files were limited in their visual presentation and it was hard to make adjustments after they were generated. A key benefit of publishing XML with InDesign is that the full range of typographic and layout design is available. After XML is created in InDesign, tracking, hyphenation, and other controls can be applied to make the XML structure into a properly typeset document. We will look at the methods you can use to get InDesign to automatically provide the right paragraph styles when importing XML. Besides InDesign's "Map Styles to Tags" and "Map Tags to Styles" dialogs, you can go further with the use of XSLT and the "namespaced" XML that is part of InDesign under the hood.

About This Book and InDesign CS

The release of CS3 in May 2007 occurred almost simultaneously with the first publication of this book, which was originally published as an O'Reilly Short Cut. I wrote the first version of the book based on CS2 and CS3. In 2010, I updated the content for CS5. In this new version, I have updated the information and screenshots for InDesign CS6.

Chief among the features introduced in CS3 and retained through CS6 is the ability to apply XSL transformations (XSLT) to XML when importing into or exporting from InDesign. I have included some XSLT examples in Chapter 10, but there is much more to explore, such as the ability to automate XML processes using scripts. Scripting requires advanced understanding of both XML structures and programming, so what I cover here will just provide a taste of the possibilities.

I assume that InDesign will perform virtually the same on Mac OS X as on Windows, as Adobe makes InDesign cross-platform compatible. However, only Windows was used for the development of the test materials for this publication. If you use InDesign on a Mac or in a mixed-OS environment, there is the possibility that something might not work as described in this book.

Adobe provides for forward migration—the ability to open a CS file in later versions than the one in which it was created—which appears to have no negative impact regarding XML processing. Adobe also provides backward compatibility, to some extent. You can save a CS6 file in IDML format, and most CS6 features will be available when you open the file in CS5.5. Refer to the Adobe InDesign documentation for assistance with InDesign backward-compatibility features and processes, especially the new documentation for CS6.

My intent is to help InDesign users understand how to work with XML more than to help XML users understand how to work with InDesign. Thus, I include explanations of XML that may be unnecessary for those experienced with it. I hope that XML novices will be able to follow the examples and XML experts will get ideas for venturing beyond the examples on their own.

Conventions Used in This Book

The following typographical conventions are used in this book:

Italic
> Indicates new terms, URLs, email addresses, filenames, and file extensions.

`Constant width`
> Used for program listings, as well as within paragraphs to refer to program elements such as variable or function names, databases, data types, environment variables, statements, and keywords.

Constant width bold

    Shows commands or other text that should be typed literally by the user.

Constant width italic

    Shows text that should be replaced with user-supplied values or by values determined by context.

    This icon signifies a tip, suggestion, or general note.

    This icon indicates a warning or caution.

Using Code Examples

This book is here to help you get your job done. In general, if this book includes code examples, you may use the code in your programs and documentation. You do not need to contact us for permission unless you're reproducing a significant portion of the code. For example, writing a program that uses several chunks of code from this book does not require permission. Selling or distributing a CD-ROM of examples from O'Reilly books does require permission. Answering a question by citing this book and quoting example code does not require permission. Incorporating a significant amount of example code from this book into your product's documentation does require permission.

We appreciate, but do not require, attribution. An attribution usually includes the title, author, publisher, and ISBN. For example: "*XML and InDesign* by Dorothy J. Hoskins (O'Reilly). Copyright 2013 Dorothy Hoskins, 978-1-449-34416-0."

If you feel your use of code examples falls outside fair use or the permission given above, feel free to contact us at *permissions@oreilly.com*.

Safari® Books Online

 Safari Books Online (*www.safaribooksonline.com*) is an on-demand digital library that delivers expert content in both book and video form from the world's leading authors in technology and business.

Technology professionals, software developers, web designers, and business and creative professionals use Safari Books Online as their primary resource for research, problem solving, learning, and certification training.

Safari Books Online offers a range of product mixes and pricing programs for organizations, government agencies, and individuals. Subscribers have access to thousands of books, training videos, and prepublication manuscripts in one fully searchable database from publishers like O'Reilly Media, Prentice Hall Professional, Addison-Wesley Professional, Microsoft Press, Sams, Que, Peachpit Press, Focal Press, Cisco Press, John Wiley & Sons, Syngress, Morgan Kaufmann, IBM Redbooks, Packt, Adobe Press, FT Press, Apress, Manning, New Riders, McGraw-Hill, Jones & Bartlett, Course Technology, and dozens more. For more information about Safari Books Online, please visit us online.

How to Contact Us

Please address comments and questions concerning this book to the publisher:

O'Reilly Media, Inc.
1005 Gravenstein Highway North
Sebastopol, CA 95472
800-998-9938 (in the United States or Canada)
707-829-0515 (international or local)
707-829-0104 (fax)

We have a web page for this book, where we list errata, examples, and any additional information. You can access this page at *http://oreil.ly/xml_and_indesign*.

To comment or ask technical questions about this book, send email to *bookquestions@oreilly.com*.

For more information about our books, courses, conferences, and news, see our website at *http://www.oreilly.com*.

Find us on Facebook: *http://facebook.com/oreilly*

Follow us on Twitter: *http://twitter.com/oreillymedia*

Watch us on YouTube: *http://www.youtube.com/oreillymedia*

Contributor

Giuseppe (Peppo) Bonelli contributed code examples for an ICML (InCopy) file generated from DocBook XML with XSLT; see Chapter 10 in this book. Peppo is a freelance consultant who specializes in helping publishers implementing processes, tools, and procedures to enable effective and sustainable cross-media publishing. He has a background in physics; lives in Milan, Italy; and has been implementing XML workflows for publishers since the end of the last century. You can contact him at *peppo.bonelli@gmail.com*.

Acknowledgments

My friend and co-developer, Terry Badger, has helped me try out many ideas for XML, ICML, and XSLT.

My thanks to the great team I worked with at Monroe Community College when I first tried to import XML into InDesign: Carol, Bob, Janet, Vince, and Sean.

As always, my gratitude for the support of Geoffrey and our sons Matt and Dana, who have listened to more about XML and InDesign over the years than they ever intended.

CHAPTER 1

A Brief Foray into Structured Content (a.k.a. XML)

Whenever we talk about eXtensible Markup Language (XML), we are talking about a type of *structured content*. In case you haven't been exposed to these concepts, let's take a brief look at them before we dive further into XML and InDesign.

The first XML concept is that of *structure*, sometimes called "hierarchy." Structure is the organization of pieces of information into a grouping that makes sense to humans. For example, if you are going to describe a course within a college course catalog, at minimum you would give the course name and a brief description. To relate this course to the larger picture of getting a degree, you would provide information about the major that the course is part of, how many credit hours the course counts for, and the prerequisites, if there are any.

Looked at from the top down, a college offers programs of study consisting of courses in a sequence. Course credits have to add up to the required number for the degree program.

If you draw the relationships as boxes that contain information, you might see that a program of study contains a set of repeating information blocks consisting of blocks of course names and descriptions, as in Figure 1-1.

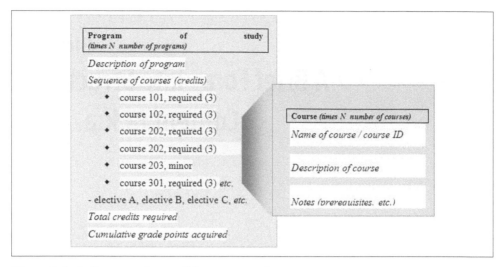

Figure 1-1. A diagram of a possible course catalog structure

Each piece of information that we want to identify and work with is given an element name. The top-level element (root) at the left of Figure 1-1 is named <Programs of Study> and consists of many individual <ProgramOfStudy> elements. Repeating element blocks make up a <CourseSequence> element.

The names of elements can be very wordy to ensure that humans can read and understand what they mean, or they can be tersely named, like Prg, Crs, and TCrd, if mostly computer programs use them. XML element naming is dependent on the person or machine who has to work with the XML and how. Here are some general naming rules: element names can't start with a number, can't contain spaces, and can't contain certain "illegal" characters such as ?, >, &, and /.

The second XML concept is *semantics*, which is applying names to things so that they are meaningful to you and others. So rather than Titlemain, Titlesub, and List, you would use names that relate to the type of information you are organizing: ProgramName, ProgramDescription, ProgramRequirements, CourseName, CourseDescription, Credits, and so on.

Hierarchy and semantics are combined in structured content and can be translated into an abstract model of XML elements, such as in Example 1-1.

Example 1-1. A tree diagram of possible course catalog structure

```
ProgramsOfStudy
↳   ProgramOfStudy
       ↳   ProgramName
       ↳   ProgramDescription
       ↳   CourseSequence
              ↳   CourseDescriptions
```

```
↳  CourseDescription_Major
    ↳  CourseDescription_Name
    ↳  CourseCreditsHrs
    ↳  CourseDescription_Text
    ↳  CourseDescription_Fotnote
↳  CourseDescription_Minor
    ↳  CourseDescription_Name
    ↳  CourseCreditsHrs
    ↳  CourseDescription_Text
    ↳  CourseDescription_Fotnote
↳  ProgramRequirements
↳  TotalProgramCredits
↳  CumulativeGradePointAverage
```

If a structure of meaningful components will be used by more than one person or organization, it can be formalized with a set of rules, such as:

Every program of study must consist of a sequence of more than one of each of required major courses, required minor courses, and elective courses. Additionally, the course credit hours must add up to the total credit hours required to complete the program of study, and the grades received must cumulatively add up to the minimum grade average for the student to graduate.

A set of rules for the structured content is called a schema or a *Document Type Definition (DTD)*. The rules can be simple or complex, depending upon the number of elements and how they can be used (whether required or optional, how many times the element can occur, and within what contexts, etc.).

Rather than spend a lot of time exploring XML and DTDs at this point, I will consider them to be part of the problem-solving process for creating a content creation and publishing workflow. There are many resources for learning about XML and DTDs online.

The key points to keep in mind are what you call the pieces of content (the element names) and how they are organized (the structure). These points are factors in setting up your InDesign import and export processes. The names of your elements can be the same as, or different from, the names of paragraph styles that you use in InDesign.

XML element attributes provide additional information, typically to enable finer distinctions among content that is basically the same. For example, in a staff directory, an attribute might be used to indicate a department head, so that when the person's name is shown, their name gets special typographical treatment in InDesign.

Unless you are using a DTD or schema developed by someone else, you can name elements and attributes in ways that are meaningful for your organization. That's why XML is "extensible"—you are not limited to a defined set of elements as you would be with HTML for web pages.

If you are using a DTD or schema provided by another organization, you will have to learn how the elements and attributes in it create the kind of structure that you will work with in InDesign. I'll examine elements and attributes and their naming more in subsequent chapters.

CHAPTER 2

InDesign XML Publishing: College Catalog Case Study

Most people look at InDesign as a layout tool for highly styled graphic designs that are rich with color and typographic controls. Some users also import data into tables or export InDesign as HTML. InDesign CS is fully capable of all these things, but if a person is exploring XML, it is usually because someone has said, "Hey, we need to use XML so that we can make web pages and PDFs and everything out of the same content." Perhaps the organization is already using XML for the website, and someone has seen that In-Design can work with XML. Or someone has used InDesign and is wondering how to extract the content from InDesign in a way that a web service or other application can use it.

In any event, although InDesign can do some pretty useful XML importing and ex-porting, Adobe does not see this as a feature intended for typical users. Their demos are business card templates and cookbooks; making XML that will match what another application or process uses is not the focus of their examples. However, Adobe has provided a number of features in InDesign for importing, creating, and exporting XML.

To get the most of the XML capabilities of InDesign, think about the bigger issues of the processes you have in place, the workflow that will help with it, and whether you need to create XML from content you already have in InDesign (that is, to export XML), to create InDesign documents from XML (that is, to import XML), or to do both of these processes (that is, bidirectional XML import/export).

As an example, I will use an actual project that needed both import and export: a college course catalog. The course catalog consists of a number of chapters, including topics such as:

- General information about the college, its history, and its program emphasis, as well as its academic calendar

- Financial aid, admissions criteria, and the application process

- Programs of study

- Course descriptions

- Student services, the regulations handbook, and policies and procedures

- Faculty and staff listing, directory, and campus maps

Of these chapters, some financial aid data, the course descriptions, and the programs of study were stored in database tables. The content of the database was published directly to the college website as HTML pages using Microsoft Active Server Pages (ASP). The rest of the content was created by staff members who sent Word documents to the InDesign layout person; these documents did not exist in the database as text entries. The InDesign files were used primarily for the printed output, a bound paper catalog.

The goal was to make the database a "single source," with the website and the printed catalog being two outputs from the same content. To synchronize the current processes, content in InDesign would be added to the database, and content from the database would be passed into InDesign.

We were dealing with two different types of content in the catalog: some could be assigned neatly to table rows and cells in a database, and some was more narrative or organized in topics. Each of these types of content needed its own analysis and design process to achieve the XML import/export. Key issues and proposed solutions were:

- Database content was extracted as plain text (separated into paragraphs) and given to the layout person in one large .txt file. The layout person imported the plain text and then had to mark up every paragraph with the correct InDesign paragraph style. Because about two-thirds of the catalog content was in the database, this meant that the layout person was manually marking up more than 130 pages of the catalog. The proposed solution was to provide database content to the layout person such that it would format itself automatically upon import into InDesign.

- All of the text about admissions, policies, registration, regulations, and personnel was being created in Word documents. These documents were imported as source material for the InDesign catalog. The text then was edited in InDesign and was finally added to the database and website via cut-and-paste operations from RTF files exported from InDesign. There were problems with getting changes on time and mistakes in editing that led to differences in the text outputs. The proposed solution was to provide the output to the database and website developers such that it could be imported as rich text "blobs" but still have some semantic meaning that would assist in locating and reusing it. After the initial import into the database, the database programmer would provide a web-based form for editing so that the database would be the ongoing "single source" for this content.

Both of these processes involved InDesign's XML capabilities, as you will see.

The database programmer and the InDesign layout person provided input on how they viewed the content, how they worked with it, and what problems they found when interchanging the content between the two applications. The editorial staff for the catalog also contributed input regarding how they reviewed and made corrections to the catalog during the publishing process.

Data-Like Content Example: The Course Description XML

The data table that contained the course descriptions was one of the largest in the database. Hundreds of course descriptions were managed in it, containing data in a regular format, as in Table 2-1.

Table 2-1. Database fields for course descriptions

Course major	Course number	Course name	Course credits	Course description	Notes
Accounting	ACC 101	Accounting Principles I	4	Basic principles of financial accounting for the business enterprise with emphasis on the valuation of business assets, measurement of net income, and double-entry techniques for recording transactions. Introduction to the cycle of accounting work, preparation of financial statements, and adjusting and closing procedures. Four class hours.	Prerequisite: MTH 098 or MTH 130 or equivalent.

In InDesign, we wanted the content to look like Figure 2-1.

There are four InDesign paragraph styles defined for the content:

Course Descriptions—Major
> The heading for the major under which the course falls.

Course Descriptions—Name
> The bold text for the course number, official name, and credits awarded, in a single line.

Course Descriptions—Text
> The normal text for the description of the course, as a paragraph.

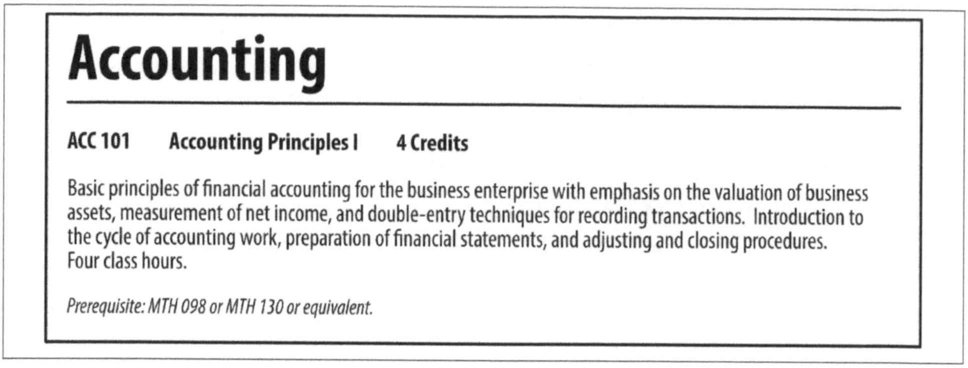

Accounting

ACC 101   Accounting Principles I   4 Credits

Basic principles of financial accounting for the business enterprise with emphasis on the valuation of business assets, measurement of net income, and double-entry techniques for recording transactions. Introduction to the cycle of accounting work, preparation of financial statements, and adjusting and closing procedures. Four class hours.

Prerequisite: MTH 098 or MTH 130 or equivalent.

Figure 2-1. Example of formatted XML output for course descriptions

Course Descriptions—Footnote

> The italic footnote, which includes prerequisites, limitations on registration, required approvals, and the like. There could be more than one paragraph of footnotes for a course.

Naming all of the paragraph styles with the same beginning keeps them together in the InDesign paragraph styles palette.

Data Exported as XML

When we exported the course description content from the database, we combined a few of the data fields (the course name and number and credits became a single element, with tabs separating the values) to align better with what the InDesign layout would be. Example 2-1 shows how the elements of a course description were written in our XML.

Example 2-1. Sample XML structure based on database fields

```
<CourseDescription_Major>Accounting</CourseDescription_Major>
<CourseDescription_Name>ACC 101&#9;Accounting Principles I&#9;4 Credits
</CourseDescription_Name>
<CourseDescription_Text>Basic principles of financial accounting for the business
enterprise with emphasis on the valuation of business assets, measurement of net
income, and double-entry techniques for recording transactions.  Introduction to
the cycle of accounting work, preparation of financial statements, and adjusting
and closing procedures.  Four class hours.</CourseDescription_Text>
<CourseDescription_Footnote type="prereq">
Prerequisite: MTH 098 or MTH 130 or equivalent.</CourseDescription_Footnote>
```

The "Notes" content from the database entry for a course was named <CourseDescrip tion_Footnote> so that it could be recognized as a specific type of note. <CourseDe scription_Footnote> was given an attribute named type, which is used generally as an indication of a prerequisite for the course, if there is one.

This approach allowed for notes that pertain to prerequisites to be searched for within the XML content.

Modeling the Structure for the Import XML

A simple DTD for the course descriptions data was generated from the XML that we extracted from the database. All of the course description elements are wrapped together in a root element named `CourseDescriptions`:

```
<?xml version="1.0" encoding="UTF-8"?>
<!-- DTD generated from database XML content using XML Spy -->
<!ELEMENT CourseDescriptions (CourseDescription_Major* |
    CourseDescription_Name* | CourseDescription_Text* |
    CourseDescription_Footnote*)+>
<!ELEMENT CourseDescription_Major (#PCDATA)>
<!ELEMENT CourseDescription_Name (#PCDATA)>
<!ELEMENT CourseDescription_Text (#PCDATA)>
<!ELEMENT CourseDescription_Footnote (#PCDATA)>
<!ATTLIST CourseDescription_Footnote
    type CDATA #REQUIRED>
```

We could have wrapped the basic structure of each course with all its fields inside an element named <CourseDescription>, but InDesign works best with XML that doesn't have many levels of content hierarchy. So we arbitrarily made this structure simple to make it easier for the InDesign layout person.

With a simple DTD and an understanding of the basic XML structure and the paragraph styles that we were going to use in InDesign, our prep work for this import was done. We'll dive into the details of the import and paragraph styles mapping later. (If you want to understand DTDs better, search for "XML DTD basics" online.)

Topical Content: The Handbook XML

We needed to reverse the process when we wanted to export the XML from InDesign to put into the database. We started by looking at the content in InDesign, thought about how we were going to store it in the database, and designed the XML markup that would achieve our goals.

Evaluating the Handbook Text for Structure

The text in the handbook was organized into topics:

- Rights and Freedoms of Students
- Code of Conduct
- Grievance Procedure
- Parking Regulations

- Alcohol and Drug Policies

Some of these topics included many subtopics, some included procedures, and some included reference tables or illustrations. Compared with the database content, this content was much more freeform and harder to predict, so the XML structure had to be more generic.

To make XML that would be useful for the particular workflow of this college, we determined that we would make each main text topic flow into an XML file, which would be changed into a rich text blob in the database (because that would be the most editable form of the content for the future editing cycles).

Modeling the Structure as a Set of Topics

The content was usually edited as a single "story" or text flow in InDesign. Some of these were small and simple enough to be made into a very shallow structure: a <Story> element that contained an optional <IntroBlock> element, at least one <Section Head>, some <SubsectionHead>s, <Subhead>s, and <para>s and optional <listitem> and <table> elements. The most complex content might include a number of topics inside a story, with the same basic headings, paragraphs, lists and tables inside a topic. We decided that content should generally be no more than three levels deep inside a story or a topic.

Our basic structure for these types of content is captured in a tree diagram as shown here:

```
Story
    @name
 ↳  IntroBlock
    ↳  para
 ↳  SectionHead
    ↳  SubSectionHead
        ↳  Subhead
            ↳  keyword
        ↳  para
            ↳  keyword
        ↳  listitem
        ↳  Table
            ↳  Cell
        ↳  keyword
        ↳  topic
            @title
            ↳  para
                ↳  keyword
            ↳  listitem
            ↳  keyword
            ↳  Table
                ↳  Cell
```

We used names of existing paragraph styles for a few elements, and kept their capitalization, such as `<SectionHeading>`, while we lowercased all the more generic elements, such as `<para>`. This made it easier to remember which element names originated from the InDesign layout.

A few elements and attributes were designed to help us manage or search the content after export. There is an attribute, `name`, for a `<Story>` element to give us a handle on the kind of information contained in a Story, such as "Career and Transfer Programs, Certificates and Advisement." A similar attribute, `title`, was used on a `<topic>` element, so that we could identify the information in a topic even if it did not have a heading to display. The `<keyword>` element could be used inside a `<Subhead>` or `<para>` element.

We did not have to be very rigorous in developing our structure. We selected names that were quite generic and flattened out structures for which we didn't think "wrapper elements" would be necessary. For example, we did not wrap a set of `<listitem>` elements in a `<list>` element. Although such an approach is common in HTML, it would be unnecessary in tagging text in InDesign, where we want the closest match we can get between the incoming elements and the number of paragraph styles that we will use. (Adobe has a similar strategy in regard to tables, having decided to dispense with `<Row>` and just use `<Table>` and `<Cell>` elements.)

With this basic structure converted into a DTD, we were ready to start marking up InDesign content as XML and validating it.

Iteration and Refinement

We didn't get the structure that we used on the first try. The first versions of the XML structure were more granular (had more little elements within the `<topic>` and the `<para>` level of structure) and had many more "wrapper elements." We tested by importing XML with various structures and different settings of the Import Options dialog to see what results we got in InDesign. If we didn't like the results, we changed the structure and tried again. When we were finished with this process, I generated a DTD from our final XML and used that DTD for validating the content.

 In Chapter 8, you will see why I prefer to go with the minimum of structural rules and to develop DTDs after creating working examples of content (if you are "rolling your own" DTD). In the example project, we only had to be sure that one InDesign layout person and one database developer would be able to understand how to create, manage, and interchange a specific set of content elements.

Net Results: Vast Improvements in Understanding and Speed

We had a lot of successes with our project. Among the most significant were a somewhat improved understanding of the database by the publishing group and much greater understanding by the database team of the publishing process. Because the bulk of the work was going to be passing content from the database to the publishing application via XML, the database programmer was intimately involved in understanding how the layout person perceived the content and what tasks he needed to perform with the content.

Besides improved comprehension between the functional groups, there was also a very important improvement in time to delivery for the layout person. He was given a brief tutorial on XML import and adjusted paragraph style names before importing the XML. Thereafter, where once he had spent days (literally) marking up the 130 pages of plain text paragraphs, he now could import all of the content in a few minutes, watch it auto-format itself as it came in, and then page through it, applying column and page breaks as needed. *The estimated time saved in manual layout of the 130 pages was about 80 percent.*

The text that was exported as XML from InDesign was marked up by an outside vendor in order to minimize the impact on the production cycle for the catalog. The database programmer was again a critical person in the success of the process change; he figured out how to get the database (which did not store XML natively) to import XML and achieve a useful, editable set of new content pieces within the database.

Our project was stretched out over a year's publishing cycle, and we held regular meetings and used a wiki to help track progress and document the project. I consider it a successful pilot of the processes that I am describing in this book. The process has been in use for seven years (as of 2012), and the college's developers have been able to adjust the process without difficulty.

Importing XML

There are several ways to work with Adobe's XML import capabilities. We'll start with the process that has been documented in an Adobe video tutorial (*http://tv.adobe.com*).

Doing It Adobe's Way: The Placeholder Approach

Adobe expects you to create a model within your InDesign document for your XML content.[1] The model is made of placeholders, which are XML elements that indicate what the structure of the incoming XML will be and how you want it to look.

This is a very sensible approach when you are starting out with XML and want to get a feel for how the imported XML will be formatted in InDesign. See Figure 3-1.

> If you import XML without any preexisting maps for paragraph styles, all the imported content will look like the default style that you get when you make a new paragraph without applying a style to it (the Basic Paragraph style).

Let's walk through the steps of the placeholder approach, using the course description content.

---

1. See "Create placeholders for repeating content" (*http://www.adobe.com/designcenter-archive/indesign/articles/indcs2at_placeholder.html*) on Adobe's website for a tutorial on placeholders. Or refer to "Format XML data in an InDesign template" (*http://users.metropolia.fi/~karita/2010-XMLandMCP/InDesign/idsn2importxml.pdf*) for an approach that is slightly different from what is described in this book.

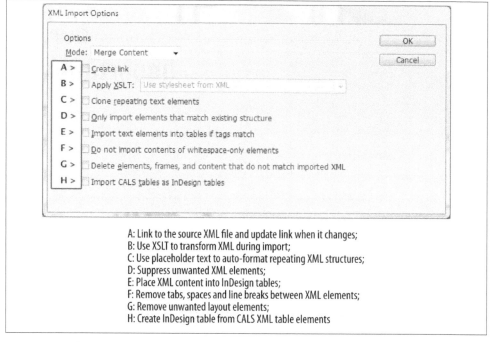

A: Link to the source XML file and update link when it changes;
B: Use XSLT to transform XML during import;
C: Use placeholder text to auto-format repeating XML structures;
D: Suppress unwanted XML elements;
E: Place XML content into InDesign tables;
F: Remove tabs, spaces and line breaks between XML elements;
G: Remove unwanted layout elements;
H: Create InDesign table from CALS XML table elements

Figure 3-1. The XML Import Options dialog with annotations

Modeling the XML You Want

Getting some structure into InDesign

The basis of your modeling will be a set of XML elements from an existing DTD or XML file. If you have XML based upon a DTD, start by importing the DTD[2] into InDesign:

1. In your InDesign document, select View→Structure or click the Structure pane icon <|> in the very far bottom-left corner of the document window.

2. Select Structure→Load DTD and then browse to select the DTD for your XML content. Click OK and a DOCTYPE declaration will appear at the top of the Structure pane (Figure 3-2).

Now we need to work with the Tags window; select Window→Tags. Because you just imported a DTD, the Tags window is populated with the element names from your DTD. See Figure 3-2.

---

2. InDesign CS2 through CS6 do not provide XML schema support. You can convert a schema to a DTD with XML Spy, Oxygen Editor, and other XML tools.

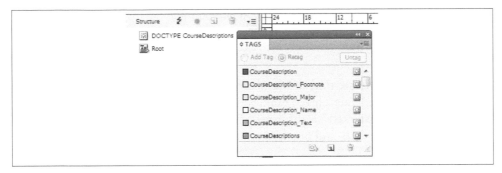

Figure 3-2. The Structure pane (top left) showing the DTD (as a DOCTYPE declaration), and the Tags window (right) showing the element names from the DTD. The DOCTYPE determines what tag names will be seen in the Tags list. Root is the default tag in any InDesign file even when no text has been tagged in the file.

If you don't have a DTD, you can load the structure directly from an XML file by importing the XML file:

1. Open the Tags palette from the Windows dropdown, then click the small arrow in the upper right of the Tags window to get the Tags menu.

2. Select Load Tags, and then browse to the XML file that you will use as a source for your XML import.

3. Select it and click OK. Element names will appear in the Tags window.

Create placeholders for XML elements

Get a text frame by clicking on the T icon and then onto your empty document. Drag out a text frame large enough to work in. Now you can start making your placeholder text in the text frame.

Choose a "wrapper" element that all of the other elements will reside within. If you imported a DTD, that will be the root element of your DTD, which in the case of my simple example is <CourseDescriptions>:

```
<?xml version="1.0" encoding="UTF-8"?>
<!ELEMENT CourseDescriptions (CourseDescription+)>
<!ELEMENT CourseDescription (CourseDescription_Major | CourseDescription_Name
| CourseDescription_Text | CourseDescription_Footnote)+>
<!ELEMENT CourseDescription_Footnote (#PCDATA)>
<!ATTLIST CourseDescription_Footnote
    type CDATA #REQUIRED>
<!ELEMENT CourseDescription_Major (#PCDATA)>
<!ELEMENT CourseDescription_Name (#PCDATA)>
<!ELEMENT CourseDescription_Text (#PCDATA)>
```

To start your placeholder XML, apply the root element tag:

1. Highlight the text frame and click the corresponding root tag name in the Tag palette.

2. Within the View menu, find the Structure item and expand it. Toggle to "Show Tagged Frames", if "Hide Tagged Frames" is displayed. Toggle to "Show Tag Markers", if "Hide Tag Markers" is displayed. This step will provide color-coded backgrounds on text frames and brackets around elements to help you see tags when you apply them.

3. Type the name of each element of your XML structure on a single line *in the order that they should appear in the document*. For the example, that means typing the following element names:

```
CourseDescription_Major
CourseDescription_Name
CourseDescription_Text
CourseDescription_Footnote
```

4. Tag each line of text with the matching XML tag by clicking the corresponding name in the Tags palette. It should look like Figure 3-3.

5. Save your file.

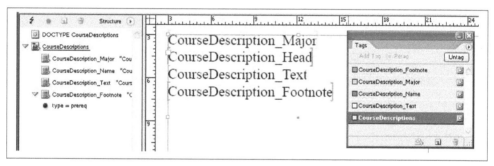

Figure 3-3. The Structure pane (left) reflects the organization of the elements and attributes of the XML. Colored brackets around each tag in the text frame (center) correspond to the color of the tag in the Tags palette (right).

Creating test XML

You can work faster if you use a small XML file for testing. Open the XML you want to import in an XML or text editor and trim it down to just a few sets of repeating content. For our example, that would be a `<CourseDescription_Major>` such as Accounting and a couple of sets of `<CourseDescription>` elements, each containing `<CourseDescription_Name>`, `<CourseDescription_Text>`, and `<CourseDescription_Footnote>` elements to make sure that the imported content has enough variation to be a good test.

If you are uncertain about editing the XML file, start by saving a copy, then remove XML elements inside the root element (do not delete the root element itself) until you have just a few blocks of content containing the element structure that you want to test. Save the trimmed file and use it for your placeholder tests.

(The more complex your XML and DTD, the larger a set of text elements you will need to cover all the possibilities of your imported XML. You can, of course, try to import the entire XML file that you plan to work with if you are feeling brave.)

If you have a DTD, but don't have the actual XML you want to import, you can create an XML file from the DTD using an application such as XML Spy or Oxygen, but you will have to create at least the amount of content that I describe (several repeating blocks of content at each level of structure that you expect to repeat).

This is what I imported into my placeholders for testing:

```
<?xml version="1.0" encoding="UTF-8" standalone="no"?>
<CourseDescriptions>
    <CourseDescription>
        <CourseDescription_Major>Accounting</CourseDescription_Major>
        <CourseDescription_Name>ACC 101&#9;Accounting Principles I&#9;4 Credits
        </CourseDescription_Name>
        <CourseDescription_Text>Basic principles of financial accounting for
        the business enterprise with emphasis on the valuation of business
        assets, measurement of net income, and double-entry techniques for
        recording transactions.  Introduction to the cycle of accounting work,
        preparation of financial statements, and adjusting and closing
        procedures. Four class hours.
        </CourseDescription_Text>
        <CourseDescription_Footnote type="prereq">Prerequisite: MTH 098 or
        MTH 130 or equivalent.</CourseDescription_Footnote>
    </CourseDescription>
    <CourseDescription>
        <CourseDescription_Name>ACC 102 Accounting Principles II&#9;4 Credits
        </CourseDescription_Name>
        <CourseDescription_Text>A continuation of the basic principles of
        financial accounting including a study of partnerships and corporation
        accounts.  The course deals with the development of accounting theory
        with emphasis onmanagerial techniques for interpretation and use of
        data in planning and controlling business activities.
        Four class hours. </CourseDescription_Text>
        <CourseDescription_Footnote type="prereq">Prerequisite: ACC 101 with a
        grade of C or higher, or ACC 110 and ACC 111 with an average grade of C
        or higher.
        </CourseDescription_Footnote>
    </CourseDescription>
    ...
</CourseDescriptions>
```

As I mentioned, we combined the values from three data fields into the single XML element named `<CourseDescription_Name>`. These values are separated by tabs (the `&#9;` seen in the code examples). This is a convenience for print publishing, where tabs are used for better readability. If you were creating a table from the XML import, you could keep these three field values distinct by making each one an XML element and applying formatting to create table cells from the imported XML. We'll look at tables in some detail later.

Importing XML into Placeholders

To import the XML:

1. Select the text frame, then the File menu, and select Import XML in the drop-down menu; the Import XML dialog box (Figure 3-4) will appear.

2. Browse to your sample XML file and select it, then check the boxes beside "Show XML Import Options" and "Import Into Selected Element" and the radio button beside Merge Content.

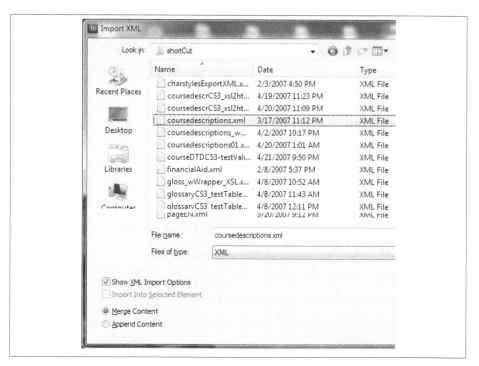

Figure 3-4. The Import XML dialog

3. Check the boxes for "Create link" and "Clone repeating text elements" and then click OK (Figure 3-5).

Figure 3-5. The Import Options dialog (InDesign CS6)

Your XML content will now appear in the Structure pane (Figure 3-6) to the left of your InDesign document pane. The text of the first part of the XML should fill the text frame on your page. It will all look like the Basic Paragraph style of the InDesign document at this point.

4. Save your InDesign file to preserve its current state before you add styles.

By default, the imported XML is collapsed in the Structure pane view. You can click on the triangles next to elements to expand them and see what other elements they contain. (A bold black dot and text below an element indicates the presence of an attribute, a bit of extra information about the element's meaning or usage.)

For sanity during editing, you may wish to expand only a small amount of XML at a time in the Structure pane. InDesign "remembers" all of the XML elements you expand during a session, so if you collapse an element and later expand it, whatever elements were expanded within it will still be expanded.

 When you have a lot of XML in a file, it can become very confusing to relate where you are in the Structure pane to where the text of the element appears in the text flow. You can highlight an element in the Structure pane, then use the Structure pane menu (upper-right corner) and select "Go to Item" to highlight the location of an XML element in the text flow.

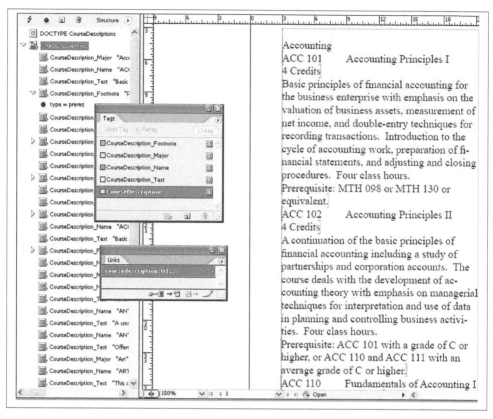

Figure 3-6. The Structure pane showing the imported XML file (expanded) at left; the Tags palette and Links palette (center) and the document with the text frame filled with the content of the XML elements (right)

Adding style to the XML elements

Now that you have imported the XML, you need to make it look how you want it to look, which means that you need to assign the appropriate paragraph style to each type of content. Fortunately, Adobe provides an easy way to apply the paragraph styles. First, you must create these, and it's a good idea to base them on the names of your XML elements:

1. In the Paragraph palette, create one new paragraph style for each of the elements except the root element, naming each one exactly as the XML elements are named.

2. Give each style distinct fonts, weight, and so on so that you can easily see the differences between them when you apply them to the text in your text frame. (If you need information on creating new paragraph styles, see the InDesign Help files.) Now you can map these new paragraph styles to your XML elements.

Alternatively, you can import styles from an existing InDesign document, and rename them if necessary.

Mapping styles to tags

You are ready to map tags to styles. At the upper-right edge of the Structure pane is a button that expands to a menu. To map the styles to tags:

1. In this menu, select Map Tags to Styles and a dialog will open (Figure 3-7).

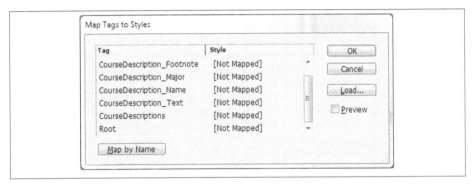

Figure 3-7. The Map Styles to Tags dialog, before mapping

2. Review the names of the elements and the names of your paragraph styles. If they match exactly (case matters!), click Map By Name. (If they do not match, change the names of the paragraph styles, not the XML tags, and then click Map By Name.)

    The dialog should now show the names aligned as shown in Figure 3-8.

 If the Tag names do not map when you click Map By Name, use the Style dropdown to the right of each tag name to select the matching paragraph style. Usually, if they do not match, it is because you have used spaces in the paragraph style names (spaces are not allowed in XML element names) or capitalization is different.

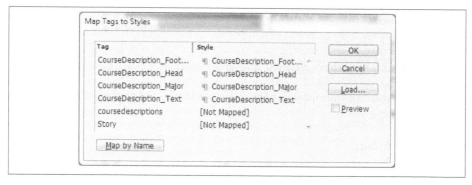

Figure 3-8. The Map Styles to Tags dialog, after mapping

3. Click OK. You will see that the text in the text frame is now styled with your paragraph styles, as in Figure 3-9. (This is typically the moment when you involuntarily cheer, or possibly leap from your chair!) Save your file.

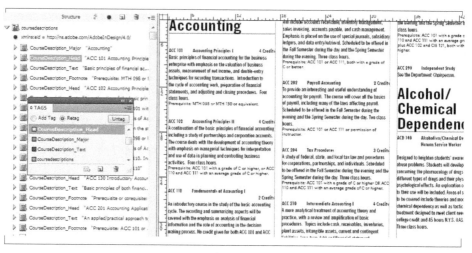

Figure 3-9. Imported XML, auto-formatted when imported into InDesign

You can look at the imported, formatted XML in your text frame and compare it to your original XML to make sure that the mapping has applied styles as you intended (see Figure 3-10).

Accounting

ACC 101   **Accounting Principles I**   **4 Credits**
Basic principles of financial accounting for the business enterprise with emphasis on the valuation of business assets, measurement of net income, and double-entry techniques for recording transactions. Introduction to the cycle of accounting work, preparation of financial statements, and adjusting and closing procedures. Four class hours.
Prerequisite: MTH 098 or MTH 130 or equivalent.

ACC 102   **Accounting Principles II**   **4 Credits**
A continuation of the basic principles of financial accounting including a study of partnerships and corporation accounts. The course deals with the development of accounting theory with emphasis on managerial techniques for interpretation and use of data in planning and controlling business

```
<coursedescriptions>
<CourseDescription_Major>Accounting
</CourseDescription_Major>
    <CourseDescription_Head>ACC
101&#9;Accounting Principles I&#9;4
Credits</CourseDescription_Head>
        <CourseDescription_Text>Basic principles
of financial accounting for the business
enterprise with emphasis on the valuation of
business assets, measurement of net income,
and double-entry techniques for recording
transactions. Introduction to the cycle of
accounting work, preparation of financial
statements, and adjusting and closing
procedures. Four class
hours.</CourseDescription_Text>
        <CourseDescription_Footnote>Prerequisite:
MTH 098 or MTH 130 or
equivalent.</CourseDescription_Footnote>
        <CourseDescription_Head >ACC
102&#9;Accounting Principles II&#9;4
Credits</CourseDescription_Head>
        <CourseDescription_Text>A continuation of
the basic principles of financial accounting
including a study of partnerships and
corporation accounts. The course deals with
the development of accounting theory with
emphasis on managerial techniques for
interpretation and use of data in planning and
controlling business activities. Four class
hours.</CourseDescription_Text>
```

Figure 3-10. The formatted XML in InDesign (left) compared with the raw XML (right)

You can adjust tabs, change colors and fonts, and make whatever changes you want to a character or paragraph style, and the changes will automatically be applied to every element (tag) with a name that matches the style.

You can also apply local overrides to the style of a particular piece of tagged text, and it will not affect the rest of the elements with the tag name that are mapped to the same paragraph style.

Now you can go whole hog with the entire XML file.

Importing the "real" XML file

Now that you've got a good working sample, you're ready to try the full XML file:

1. Select the root node of your sample XML file in the Structure pane.

2. Delete the file. A dialog will appear asking for confirmation that you want to take this action; click Delete.

3. Import XML as before, but select the real XML file you want to publish, rather than your sample file. Select Merge to replace the empty root element with the new XML. You can see the styled text reappear in the text frame, and many more XML elements will appear in the Structure pane.

There may be a delay while the Import Options dialog processes the XML file when you import something larger than the sample file we have used so far. In the case of very large XML files, InDesign will occasionally crash. If that happens, consider breaking the XML file up into a few smaller files and choose to Append each one on import, rather than Merge, so that they will appear in the text flow in the order that you append them.

XML is memory-intensive. If you are short on memory (and money to upgrade your hardware) and your documents are freezing, consider saving a large document as several smaller ones and putting them together with the Book feature in InDesign. See your InDesign documentation for information on Books.

If you want to see exactly where the tags appear around the text in your file, you can inspect them with the Story Editor. Under the Edit menu, choose "Edit in Story Editor". Each piece of tagged text in the flow will appear with the angle symbols around it, color-coded to the Tag color. In InDesign, paragraph breaks appear after the ending angle symbols. See Figure 3-11.

Figure 3-11. The Story Editor showing tag markers (angle symbols) around tagged text

If you put a line break or tab inside the tag markers of an XML tag, these will be treated as normal tabs and paragraph breaks by InDesign.

If you remove the line break between two tags, the content will run together in a single paragraph.

Scroll down through the file and look at the tags. If something appears to have been tagged incorrectly, you can select it, and then click a different tag name in the Tag palette. You can also drag elements into a different order if the order is wrong (for example, moving the footnote in Figure 3-11 to the position after the description text).

Once you are satisfied that the tagging is correct, use the Edit menu to switch back to Edit in Layout. Now you can make additional text frames and flow the text as you would normally flow any text in your InDesign layout. (If you need assistance in setting up text frames and flowing text, see the InDesign Help files.)

Use autoflow to fill threaded frames that run from page to page.

With InDesign CS4 and later versions, you can use Smart Text Reflow features to add pages full of content to your document automatically. In CS2 or CS2, add pages and then thread more frames to continue the flow of XML.

An Aside: The Scary "Map Styles to Tags" Dialog Message

When you were using "Map Tags to Styles", you might have noticed an option to "Map Styles to Tags". If you choose "Map Styles to Tags", the dialog for mapping looks very similar, but you will see a message on it (Figure 3-12) that may give you pause: "Note: Mapping styles to tags completely restructures the text in your document."

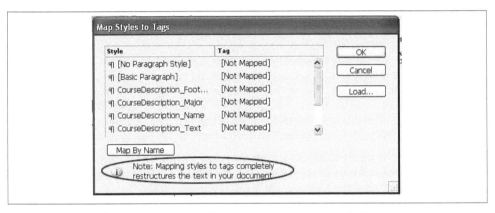

Figure 3-12. The "Map Styles to Tags" dialog (warning text circled)

Yipes! What does that mean? Adobe is warning you that these mappings are going to apply *all across your current document*. If you Map by Name and the names match, and you only have content for one type of XML structure, all should be well. This dialog is generally used when you *don't* have imported XML already in your InDesign file.

Don't map the Basic Paragraph to any XML element if you want to be able to have non-XML content in the same document as your XML.

But what happens if you already have XML tags on your text and you now use "Map Styles to Tags"? If you use "Map Styles to Tags", InDesign will change your structure to match the Paragraph Styles that you select with the dialog or map by matching names, which might cause problems. If you have differences between the Paragraph Style names and the XML tag names, your XML elements will now have names that may not match your DTD. If some of the text doesn't have a corresponding XML tag, the mapping will be only partial. In either case, your XML will be invalid, a problem you might not notice until you try to export XML out of InDesign to use for another process that depends on the DTD.

Rule of thumb: Use "Map Styles to Tags" for tagging text for *exporting* XML that you have created from InDesign. Use "Map Tags to Styles" when *importing* XML to create text in your InDesign document.

Mingling Non-XML and XML Content in a Text Flow

It is possible to create a text flow that contains untagged (non-XML) content along with XML. We can have the content set up as a running text flow, with all of the courses for a major occurring one after another. We can use the same XML and include some non-XML elements as well.

The InDesign documentation describes a method for including text between XML elements that form repeating blocks. For example, you could make a set of labels that would precede each element in a block. The best way to understand this method is try it out with small sample XML files, following the instructions in the help for using placeholders with XML.

Use the repeating blocks techniques whenever your XML content has nested elements in consistent, orderly structure. *Don't* use repeating blocks when the XML content is variable in structure.

When a text flow contains both XML-tagged and normal text, you can see this text by placing the cursor in the text flow and then choosing Edit→Select All. The text in the flow will be reverse-highlighted (as shown in Figure 3-13), so it is easy to see where the flow is on the page. You can switch to Edit→Edit in Story Editor to see that the normal text has no tag markers around it (Figure 3-14).

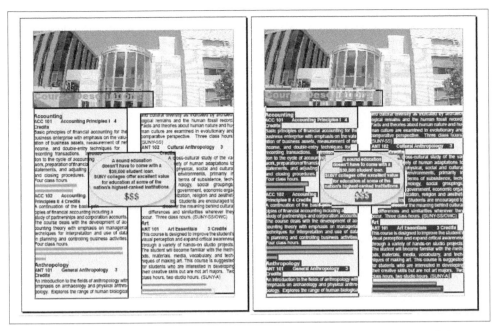

Figure 3-13. Using Select All to see where the text flow appears on the page (right)

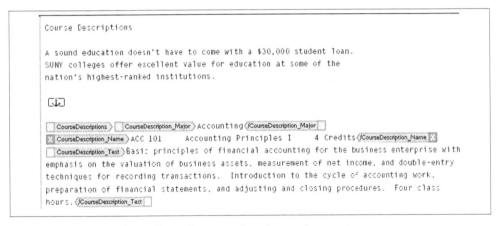

Figure 3-14. A mixed text flow of untagged and tagged content

The untagged text will be included in the XML if you export the whole mixed text flow (see Example 3-1). Manual line breaks and paragraph breaks (which may need to be stripped out later, depending on your processes) will be included in the XML output file. See "Bad Characters" (page 74) in Chapter 9 for more information.

If you use a DTD, and the DTD doesn't permit plain text within the root element or between elements, your XML will not validate. So you may have to get rid of the untagged text with a subsequent process such as an XSL transform (XSLT). An XSLT can also be used to make the un-tagged lines of text in the <Story> element into individual XML elements, such as <h1> and <p>. See Chapters 8 and 10.

Sometimes you need more than just the Export with XSLT features of InDesign to get the final XML result you want. You would start by using an XSLT during export, then use a subsequent process to apply additional transformations to the XML content until it conforms to your target DTD and validates. This situation is similar to the issues that arise when you export InDesign files to HTML or ePub formats; usually, more work is required after export to get the best quality in the output format.

Example 3-1. A sample of XML containing unmarked text (bold text between the Story and Course Descriptions elements)

```
<?xml version="1.0" encoding="UTF-8" standalone="yes"?>
<Root>
    <Story>Course Descriptions
A sound education doesn't have to come with a $30,000 student loan.
SUNY colleges offer excellent value for education at some of the
nation's highest-ranked institutions.
<CourseDescriptions>
    <CourseDescription>
        <CourseDescription_Major>Accounting</CourseDescription_Major>
        <CourseDescription_Name>
            ACC 101&#9;Accounting Principles I&#9;4 Credits
        </CourseDescription_Name>
        <CourseDescription_Text>
            Basic principles of financial accounting for the business enterprise
            with emphasis on the valuation of business assets, measurement of net
            income, and double-entry techniques for recording transactions.
            Introduction to the cycle of accounting work, preparation of
            financial statements, and adjusting and closing procedures.
            Four class hours.
        </CourseDescription_Text>
        <CourseDescription_Footnote type="prereq">
            Prerequisite: MTH 098 or MTH 130 or equivalent.
        </CourseDescription_Footnote>
    </CourseDescription>
```

Exporting XHTML When XML is in Your InDesign File

Besides "Export as XML", exporting XML-tagged content as XHTML from InDesign (as of CS4) is another option:

- *In CS6 and CS5.5*, use File→Export→HTML (which automatically makes the HTML with the namespace `<html xmlns="http://www.w3.org/1999/xhtml">`); in the resulting HTML dialog (Figure 3-15), you have the option to export HTML in Order→Same As XML Structure.

- *In CS5*, use File→Export For→Dreamweaver; then, in the XHTML dialog, you have the option to export XHTML in Order→Same As XML Structure.

- *In CS4*, it's an either-or choice: File→Export for Dreamweaver (as XHTML), or File→Export as XML.

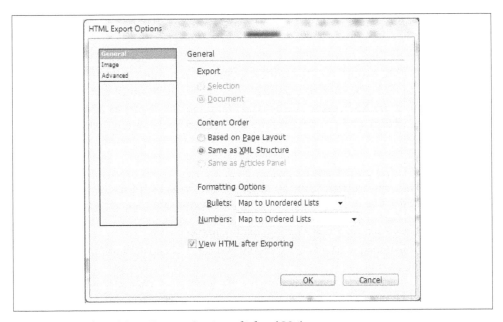

Figure 3-15. The HTML Export Options dialog (CS6)

What does exporting as (X)HTML, "Same as XML Structure" mean? Actually, it's a tip about what the HTML export generally does—all the content you have selected for exporting as HTML comes out from the top-left to the bottom-right corner of your spread in X-Y coordinate position. If you select content that is tagged in XML, then in CS5 and CS6, you can choose to use the XML order as the way your content will come out in HTML.

See Figure 3-16 for an example in which the page spread includes an image in the upper-left corner.

```
<body>
        <div id="table-list-export-as-html-recipes">
                <div class="image">
                        <img
src="table_list_export_as_HTML_recipes-
web-images/0001271_opt.jpeg" alt="missing image file" />
                </div> etc.

<body>
        <div id="table-list-export-as-html-recipes-xmlorder">
                <div class="story">
                        <table id="table-1">
<tr><td>cell 1</td><td>cell 2<td></tr>  etc.
```

Figure 3-16. Results of different (X)HTML export options; export in page order in the top <body> example, and export in XML order in the lower <body> example

This feature can be very important for saving time in web page development. If you use the standard HTML export, and the resulting content is not in the sequence that you want, you will have to drag content around in your HTML editor until you have it where you want it. But if the XML order is what you want, use the "Same as XML Structure" option in CS5 and CS6, and you can get the exact sequence of content that you want for your web page.

The export option "Same as Articles Panel" was added in InDesign CS5.5. The Articles panel and the XML structure are completely independent of each other. If you export in XML order, only XML content will be exported, with the exception that CALS tables can be created from untagged tables during export. You can add and delete XML elements, and add or delete article content, in the Structure pane or the Article panel, independent of each other. If you place a new graphic and add it to an article, but you don't also apply an XML tag, it will export with the article order setting but will not be present in exported XML.

This separation could be helpful if you want to mix XML elements with non-XML content as described in "Mingling non-XML and XML content in a text flow." You can plan a dual-purpose content that contains some elements that are untagged as XML but are included in the article, then export the content twice: once to take advantage of the XML order and once to use the article order. See also Chapter 7.

Doing It Your Way: Using the Options for Your Own Process

Import XML Using Only Merge—No Other Import Settings

You can use Import XML Options→Merge Content without any other Import Options. Merge Content replaces the contents of the selected text frame or structure element with the incoming XML content. If you have mapped tags to paragraph styles, the styles will be applied to the XML content as it is imported. Otherwise, the XML content will all look like your Basic Paragraph default style.

If you do not select a text frame when using Merge, the XML content replaces the Root element in the Structure pane. It will not flow into text frames. You can then drag elements from the Structure pane into text frames on your page to place the imported XML as you want it. If you have XML elements in your content that are not for the end user (such as metadata tags about versions or authors that only are useful to the editors and layout people), these will be included in your XML structure. If you do not drag these into text frames in your layout, they will not appear in the text flow. However, they will increase the number of elements you have to scroll through in the Structure pane. (To exclude these nonessential XML elements when importing XML in CS3, select "Only import elements that match existing structure.")

Using Append

If you want to place XML content at the end of an existing text flow, use Append instead of Merge. Append always places the new XML content at the end of the text flow, but it does *not* replace existing content when the XML is imported. You can Append several XML files in the order that you want them to appear in the text flow.

If you do not use Create Link when you import and Append, the XML files will all become part of one XML structure, but you will no longer have a way to manage them independently within InDesign.

Linking to External XML Files

InDesign treats an imported, linked XML file as it does other external files (such as image files) that are linked when imported. Be aware that linked files increase the chances of unanticipated events (crashes), even as they provide an easy way to make sure the XML in InDesign is synchronized with the source XML.

External updates on Open and using the Links palette

If you close and reopen an InDesign file with linked XML, you will get a warning dialog if the linked file is not available (has been moved or renamed since it was linked). You can navigate to a new file or a renamed file and relink by using the Links palette to refresh the XML inside InDesign. Select Window→Links, then click the name of the XML file in the list of linked assets. Click the Relink icon on the bottom edge of the Links window and select the file to which you linked.

If you use "Create link" in conjunction with Append, you can update appended parts of the imported XML structure independently.

You can choose not to link when importing XML, or unlink an XML file from its source later, if the import is a "one-time" process to start a document and you don't anticipate needing to keep synchronized with the source XML.

Creating Text Flows for the Imported XML

Once you have imported the XML, if you did not select a text frame when importing it, you can play with the layout components and organize how text will flow from one frame to another.

For a single text flow, drag the root element of your XML from the Structure pane into a text frame.

If you want part of the XML content, such as an introduction, to appear in a separate frame, create another text frame and drag the introduction elements into it from the Structure pane. Then drag the main content into its own text frame.

The Importance of "Document Order" for Imported XML

InDesign imports XML elements in the order in which they appear (this behavior may seem self-evident, but there are ways to apply XSL in conjunction with XML to change the sequence order of elements). *A structure that occurs only once in your XML file cannot appear multiple times in the InDesign layout.* So if you want a block of elements to appear multiple times, it should be repeated in the XML.

An example of this would be a Caution block, which might have the same wording every time it is used. It would be more efficient if you could drag the same structure into an anchored text frame every time you need a Caution, but InDesign will only present the structure where you first place it.

 If you drag the XML that you want to repeat into a frame on a Master page, it can "repeat" for each page that uses that Master layout, but it will not be related to the order of other XML elements in the document.

Be aware that content on master pages will not be exported as part of an ePub.

Rearranging XML elements in the structure pane

You can drag and drop elements in the Structure pane to rearrange them. Select the structure you want to move (a single element or a set of elements) and drag them into the new position.

 It is a bad idea to rearrange XML that you have imported as *linked*. There is a high likelihood of a bad crash. If you must rearrange structure in a linked XML file that you have imported, it is best to edit the file in the XML outside of InDesign. In the Link window, select the linked XML file, then click the "pencil" button to Edit Original. Depending on your settings, another application such as Dreamweaver may open, or you may have to select an application to use for XML editing. If you have nothing else, Notepad will work, but I recommend an XML-aware editor such as oXygen XML Author or TextEdit 2.

Fixing up structure in the Story Editor

Just as in the Structure pane, you can rearrange XML elements in the Story Editor view. Make sure your text cursor is inside the flow and within an XML element, then select Edit→Edit in the Story Editor. Hold down the mouse button and drag across one or more XML elements from the starting tag marker to the ending tag marker, then hold down the mouse button and drag the elements to the new position.

The benefit of editing in the Story Editor is that you can see the tag markers clearly and thus work on deeply nested elements in high detail. The drawback is that you can't expand and collapse the XML structure, so if you need to move some XML a distance from its current position, it can be hard to tell when you are getting to the location where you want to place the elements.

> **Rule of thumb:** Rearrange elements in the Structure pane when you need to work with a large section of the XML file. Use the Story Editor view if you need to move XML elements precisely and you don't have to drag them very far.

 As noted in the section "Rearranging XML elements in the structure pane" (page 33), it is bad practice to rearrange elements in a *linked* XML file.

You can use the Structure view to find an element that you want to edit. Open the Structure pane menu and select Go to Item, then select Edit→Edit in the Story Editor. The Story Editor will open the XML file at the location of the selected item (element).

One nice thing about the tag markers in Story Editor is that you cannot accidentally remove a starting or an ending tag marker from an element. The markers are artifacts of the display, not part of the text. So you are protected from creating invalid XML that doesn't have matching start and end tags.

One bad thing about the Story Editor is that it is easy to mangle the visual appearance of the text in the flow without noticing. Within an element, you can use tabs, manual line breaks or new paragraph breaks. These will then show up in the text flow when you switch back to Edit in Layout view. In some cases, this may force your XML to overflow the text frame. You won't be able to see where the end of the XML text flow is unless you extend the text frame or make a new text frame and connect it to the frame with the overflow. (If you need help with understanding frames and overflows, see the InDesign Help topics.)

It is good practice to switch back to Edit in Layout view frequently if you are editing in the Story Editor, just to make sure that you are not going to have a lot of layout problems to fix when you are finished editing the XML.

Understanding InDesign's XML Import Options

When you first encounter the XML Import Options dialog, you may have difficulty deciding which options to use.

To start with, you should know that in InDesign terminology, an "element" can be a design or layout component such as text frame, paragraph, or image, rather than an XML `<element>`. A "tag" in InDesign terms refers to a piece of content marked up with XML element name. Table 3-1 should help you use the XML Import Options dialog.

Table 3-1. Table of XML import options[a]

If your XML:	Choose this import option:	Comments
Should create an updated InDesign file when the source XML is changed	Create link	If you use this option, you can update the XML within InDesign using the Links palette, just as you would update an image or other linked file. Adobe warns that unexpected results can occur if the updated XML structure is different from what was originally imported into InDesign. Caveat emptor.
Contains repeating blocks of elements that you always want to format in the same way	Clone repeating text elements	This option is best for fast auto-formatting of XML extracted from databases, or other repeating XML structures that need consistent layout. Use with placeholders that model the exact sequence in which you want to lay out the XML content.
Contains elements that are not needed in your current InDesign document	Only import elements that match existing structure	In this case, "elements" does seem to mean XML elements, but "existing structure" refers to the tags you have set up within InDesign, not to the structure of the entire incoming XML file. Use this setting to keep the XML import free of extraneous elements such as metadata that you didn't map to paragraph styles.

If your XML:	Choose this import option:	Comments
Should create a table layout in your InDesign document (if you want to use this capability without it being obvious, make a table without any visible borders)	Import text elements into tables if tags match	If you have set up a table in your InDesign document and mapped tags to the table structure, imported XML will flow into the table cells. This feature is very powerful for formatting large tables but may not work as expected if you need nested tables. InDesign provides ways to make headers and footers for tables that run across multiple text frames, which can be used with XML import. See the separate discussion of tables in this book in the section "The Special Case of InDesign Tables (Namespaced XML)" (page 49).
Should flow around untagged elements in the InDesign document (labels, images, pulled quotes, etc.)	Do not import contents of whitespace-only elements	This, the single most confusing option, keeps untagged (non-XML) text in a text flow from being overwritten by incoming XML elements. In InDesign terms, a whitespace-only "element" does not show up in the structured pane but is visible in the Story Editor view. It is generally a tab, line break, or space(s). This option is best understood by testing. This option will insert labels when cloning repeating blocks created with the placeholders technique; it preserves untagged elements at the point where they appear in the text flow.
Contains optional structures	Delete elements, frames and content that do not match imported XML	If you are creating page layouts with tagged text frames that are not always needed on every page of similar layout, this option will remove such text frames when the XML is imported and a text frame is not needed. Adobe provides an example of a sidebar Notes text frame; when there is no corresponding Notes XML on a page, the text frame is removed from the page when the XML is imported.

^a Table 3-1 is based on "Adobe InDesign CS3 and XML: A Technical Reference" (*http://wwwimages.adobe.com/www.adobe.com/content/dam/Adobe/en/products/indesign/pdfs/indesign_and_xml_technical_reference.pdf*).

Using "Clone Repeating Text Elements"

Quick test: if you have created placeholders for your XML elements, select the placeholders, choose Merge, and import the entire XML file *without* checking the "Clone repeating text elements" option. How much of your XML file was imported?

It seems that InDesign expects that you will have a repeating type of content structure, identifiable by a "wrapper" element that contains other elements. For example, the course descriptions content has a <CourseDescription> element containing the name, description, and prerequisite content. Without the wrapper <CourseDescription> element, InDesign will not properly apply the "clone" to the incoming XML when you select the "Clone repeating text elements" option.

 It is not unusual to have to iterate on XML development processes until you achieve the desired appearance for imported XML. Try each option and document the results as you go, then make the best settings into part of your standard procedure.

To clarify, Table 3-2 contains some examples.

Table 3-2. Comparison of wrapped and unwrapped elements used as placeholders

Wrapped element structure	Unwrapped element structure
Result: "Clone repeating text elements" will work properly if placeholders were set up; every repeating structure will be formatted identically.	*Result:* Without the wrapper element `<CourseDescription>`, "Clone repeating text elements" will import only the first structure block of the XML. Subsequent blocks will not be imported or formatted.

Wrapped element structure:

```
<CourseDescription>
  <CourseDescription_Name>ACC
101&#9;Accounting Principles I&#9;4
Credits </CourseDescription_Name>
<CourseDescription_Text>Basic principles
of financial accounting for the business
enterprise with emphasis on the valuation
of business assets, measurement of net
income, and double-entry techniques for
recording transactions.  Introduction to
the cycle of accounting work, preparation
of financial statements, and adjusting and
closing procedures.
Four class hours.</CourseDescription_Text>
  <CourseDescription_Footnote
type="prereq">Prerequisite: MTH 098 or
  MTH 130 or equivalent.
  </CourseDescription_Footnote>
</CourseDescription>
<CourseDescription>
    <CourseDescription_Name>ACC 102
Accounting Principles II&#9;4 Credits
    </CourseDescription_Name>
    <CourseDescription_Text>A continuation
of the basic principles of financial
accounting including a study of
partnerships and corporation accounts.
The course deals with the development of
accounting theory with emphasis on
managerial techniques for interpretation
and use of data in planning and
controlling business activities. Four
class hours.</CourseDescription_Text>
    <CourseDescription_Footnote
type="prereq">Prerequisite: ACC 101 with a
grade of C or higher, or ACC 110 and ACC
111 with an average grade of C or higher.
    </CourseDescription_Footnote>
</CourseDescription>
```

Etc.

Unwrapped element structure:

```
<CourseDescription_Name>ACC
101&#9;Accounting Principles I&#9;4
Credits </CourseDescription_Name>
<CourseDescription_Text>Basic
principles of financial accounting
for the business enterprise with
emphasis on the valuation of
business assets, measurement of net
income, and double-entry techniques
for recording transactions.
Introduction to the cycle of
accounting work, preparation of
financial statements, and adjusting
and closing procedures.  Four class
hours.</CourseDescription_Text>
<CourseDescription_Footnote
type="prereq">Prerequisite: MTH 098
or MTH 130 or equivalent.
</CourseDescription_Footnote>
```

When "Clone repeating text elements" is used as Adobe intends, it works beautifully. (I have successfully created many pages of content with this option.)

Importing Only Elements That Match Structure

Sometimes you don't want part of the XML file to appear in the printed version of the content, such as XML elements that describe the document itself, its creator, purpose, approvals, and so on, which are commonly referred to as "metadata." If you create placeholders for all the elements that you want, but don't create placeholders for the unwanted XML elements, you can use this option to exclude them from the import.

For example, in the following XML file section, the <metadata> element is not in the placeholder structure in the InDesign document.

```
<CourseDescriptions>
<metadata><creator>Hoskins</creator><createDate>03012007</createDate><note>used
for table layout (table tagged as &lt;CourseDescriptions&gt;)</note>
<note>placeholder text is named with element names for clarity; paragraph style
names may be different, so not using Map Tags to Styles with Map by Name
checkbox.</note></metadata>
<CourseDescription_Major>Accounting</CourseDescription_Major>
<CourseDescription>
<CourseDescription_Name>ACC 101&#9;Accounting Principles I&#9;4 Credits
</CourseDescription_Name>
<CourseDescription_Text>Basic principles of financial accounting for the
business enterprise with emphasis on the valuation of business assets,
measurement of net income, and double-entry techniques for recording
transactions. Introduction to the cycle of accounting work, preparation of
financial statements,  and adjusting and closing procedures. Four class hours.
</CourseDescription_Text>
<CourseDescription_Footnote type="prereq">Prerequisite: MTH 098 or MTH 130 or
equivalent.</CourseDescription_Footnote>
</CourseDescription>
```

Because the metadata tags do not match the placeholder elements that were set up, they can be excluded using the "Import only elements that match structure" option. So the result should be only this in the imported XML:

```
<CourseDescriptions>
<CourseDescription_Major>Accounting</CourseDescription_Major>
<CourseDescription>
<CourseDescription_Name>
    ACC 101&#9;Accounting Principles I&#9;4 Credits
</CourseDescription_Name>
<CourseDescription_Text>
    Basic principles of financial accounting for the business enterprise
    with emphasis on the valuation of business assets, measurement of net
    income, and double-entry techniques for recording transactions.
    Introduction to the cycle of accounting work, preparation of financial
    statements, and adjusting and closing procedures.  Four class hours.
</CourseDescription_Text>
<CourseDescription_Footnote type="prereq">
    Prerequisite: MTH 098 or MTH 130 or equivalent.
</CourseDescription_Footnote>
</CourseDescription>
```

If the imported XML file is linked, then the XML in the original file will still contain the elements that weren't imported. They just won't be in the InDesign document structure. So don't expect to see them if you *export* the XML from InDesign later.

 If you plan to validate XML, be careful to not exclude elements that are *required* by the DTD.

Avoiding Overwriting Text Labels in the Placeholder Elements

In InDesign, a "whitespace-only" element is one that contains a tab, line break, or space(s), and if you find that difficult to understand by reading these words, you're not alone. The "Do not import contents of whitespace-only elements" option could hardly be more obtuse. In the *Adobe InDesign CS2 User Guide*, the description of this option reads:

> Leaves any existing content in place if the matching XML content contains only white-space (such as a return or tab character). Use this option if you've included text between elements that you want preserved. For example, when laying out recipes generated from a database, you might add labels, such as "Ingredients" and "Instructions." As long as the parent element that wraps each recipe contains only whitespace, InDesign leaves the label in place.[3]

I'm *sure* that clarifies how to use this option, but just in case it doesn't, let's break it down by example. Here is some XML placeholder content with labels inserted between some of the elements:

```
<CourseDescriptions>
<CourseDescription>
Major:
    <CourseDescription_Major>CourseDescriptions_Major</CourseDescription_Major>
<CourseDescription_Name>CourseDescriptions_Name</CourseDescription_Name>
<CourseDescription_Text>CourseDescriptions_Text</CourseDescription_Text>
    Note:
    <CourseDescription_Footnote>CourseDescriptions_Footnote
    </CourseDescription_Footnote>
</CourseDescription>
</CourseDescriptions>
```

Here is the XML structure that we are going to import:

```
<CourseDescriptions>
    <CourseDescription_Major>Accounting</CourseDescription_Major>
    <CourseDescription>
```

---

3. The Adobe InDesign CS3 User Guide is available from the Adobe Store online (*http://wwwimages.adobe.com/ www.adobe.com/products/indesign/scripting/pdfs/InDesign_User_Guide_XML_chapter.pdf*).

```
<CourseDescription_Name>
    ACC 101&#9;Accounting Principles I&#9;4 Credits
</CourseDescription_Name>
<CourseDescription_Text>
  Basic principles of financial accounting for the business enterprise
  with emphasis on the valuation of business assets, measurement of
  net income, and double-entry techniques for recording
  transactions. Introduction to the cycle of accounting work,
  preparation of financial statements, and adjusting and closing
  procedures. Four class hours.
</CourseDescription_Text>
<CourseDescription_Footnote type="prereq">
  Prerequisite: MTH 098 or MTH 130 or equivalent.
</CourseDescription_Footnote>
    </CourseDescription>
</CourseDescriptions>
```

If we use the "Do not import contents of whitespace-only elements" option when we import XML content into an InDesign template document with our placeholder text, the result of the import will be labeled entries in the final XML, as in the following example:

```
<CourseDescriptions>
Major:
    <CourseDescription_Major>Accounting</CourseDescription_Major>
<CourseDescription>
<CourseDescription_Name>
    ACC 101&#9;Accounting Principles I&#9;4 Credits
</CourseDescription_Name>
<CourseDescription_Text>
  Basic principles of financial accounting for the business enterprise
  with emphasis on the valuation of business assets, measurement of net
  income, and double-entry techniques for recording transactions.
  Introduction to the cycle of accounting work, preparation of financial ,
  statements and adjusting and closing procedures.  Four class hours.
</CourseDescription_Text>
    Note:
<CourseDescription_Footnote type="prereq">
  Prerequisite: MTH 098 or MTH 130 or equivalent.
</CourseDescription_Footnote>
</CourseDescription>
</CourseDescriptions>
```

This option is really useful when combined with another XML import option, "Clone repeating text elements." When these options are used together in an InDesign document that contains placeholder elements, the incoming XML elements that match the placeholder tags come into the text frame, along with the labels you created between the XML elements. So, in the InDesign layout, you get the labels, such as "Major:" and "Note:" within every repeating block, without having to type them over and over again.

To get the placeholder and cloning features to work properly, make a template (*.indt*) file of the placeholder content. Then use that template to create a new InDesign file and import the XML using "Clone repeating text elements."

Deleting Nonmatching Structure, Text, and Layout Components

The "Delete elements, frames and content that do not match imported XML" XML import option provides a way to "clean up" your layouts during import. It is very handy for getting unused layout objects off your pages. You would most likely use it when working with multiple pages that have the same layouts, as in this example, which has two columns of the major text flow (light gray areas), and text frames on the outside edge of the page that are tagged with one type of XML element as a heading for the page (green areas). When the XML is imported using "Delete elements, frames and content that do not match imported XML," the headings are placed in the text frames tagged as headings, and they do not appear in the main text flow where they occur in the document order of the XML elements. If elements flow through the main text flow for an entire page without a heading element that matches the tagged text frame at the outer page edge, the heading text frame disappears from the layout.

The page spread on the left in Figure 3-17 has two tagged text frames for headings in the outside columns. When heading elements in the incoming XML match the tag of the text frame, the text frames will be used. The first heading is placed in the text box on the lefthand page, while the second heading element is placed on the righthand page. (The original location of the heading within the XML document and the final location after import are indicated by dotted line arrows.)

The page spread on the right in Figure 3-17 has only one matching heading element, so the tagged text frame that is not needed was removed from the lefthand page of the spread when "Delete elements, frames and content that do not match imported XML" was used.

This option is very helpful for some types of layouts, but you should be aware that once unneeded text frames are removed from the layout, reimporting the XML file or updating its link will not create any new text frames on pages were they have been removed.

> ✒**Rule of thumb:** Be cautious with any option that removes objects from your layout programmatically. Be sure to save a copy of your InDesign file before you import XML using the "Delete elements, frames and content that do not match imported XML" option.

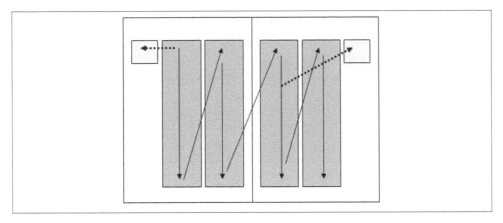

Figure 3-17. Cleaning up layouts during import

Importing Images

InDesign can import XML image information that will place an image in the layout:

- If the image will not be inline, InDesign expects an image placeholder (a graphics frame) to be tagged as an element with a *required* attribute named href. The tagged graphics frame lets you place the image in a location that is not in the main text flow.

- The value of the href attribute is the path to the local file, such as file:///C:/adobetut/pictures/ID_XML_Tutorial/Links/01_f.psd, where the linked image file resides. (Note the use of file:/// in the path.)

- In the XML file, these will be simple element structures in the form <Image href="file:///path/imagefilename1.psd"/>, <Image href="file:///path/imagefilename2.tif"/>, <Image href="file:///path/imagefilename3.ai"/>, and so on, and multiple images can be grouped inside a wrapper such as a <PictureGroup> element.

- Captions are not created inside the graphics frame but are created in separate text frames.

The only challenges I see are that you need to know the path and filename of each of the images that you want to import; so, in essence, you need to have a pretty complete layout concept ahead of importing the XML.

Images come in at their actual size, but you can shrink them to fit your graphics frame (see the Help files for information on shrinking to fit).

See also Chapter 4 for the tagging steps if you don't want to do the brief tutorial from Adobe mentioned earlier.

Despite what it says in the InDesign documentation, it didn't seem necessary to create an <Image> element for importing an inline graphic. I think the mention of tagging a graphic with an <Image> tag is to get the automatic href attribute when you are creating XML to *export* from InDesign.

You can create the required href attributes from differently named XML structures using the Apply XSLT option in the XML Import Options dialog. You would have to write an XSL template to transform the source XML element into the structure that InDesign requires. See Chapter 10 for information.

Inline Image Imports

The XML that you use to import an image inline is very simple in structure:

```
<BannerImage href="file:///images/slogan_m.gif"/>
```

(In this case, the GIF file was in an */images* folder below the folder where my InDesign document resided.)

An image that is placed inline in the XML flow can't be dragged out into a separate graphic frame after the XML is placed in the layout. To make the image float instead of inline, create a graphic frame, copy and paste the image into it, move the graphic frame where you want it, and then delete the original inline image element.

If the placeholder approach was used to make an InDesign template that included an image element as part of the placeholder content, the image elements should pop into the assigned location in the placeholder when the XML is imported. (This is how photos are added to sets of business cards in Adobe's placeholder examples.)

Tagging XML in InDesign

The Case for Tagging Content: Why You Need XML

What makes sense for you to import or export as XML should be driven by a business need. The information in the XML should be valuable enough to justify the time and effort to mark up the content as XML and export it, or to create a template to import it.

Business functions, such as sales, marketing, manufacturing, shipping, and the like rely upon documents of various kinds to transmit information. If you look at documents, you can usually discern the function the document serves and who needs to use the document. If you look closely at documents that seem fairly "freeform," such as marketing collateral, you can ferret out tidbits of discrete information within the text and images.

Try examining a piece of marketing literature and seeing what it really contains. Typically, in the small print are legal disclaimers, copyrights, trademark notices, and the like. Does the business have a way to control the wording and usage of these important pieces of content in all of their printed materials and web pages? Expensive lawsuits can result if they are left off, become outdated, or provide erroneous information.

Now look at the typical contact information and branding—company logos, slogans, addresses, phone numbers, and web, email, and street addresses. These also can differ from time to time, and from use to use, if they are retyped at the time that a marketing piece is created. Without a single source for these tidbits, there is the opportunity to omit or misspell every time a new content version is created.

If these small bits of scattered information don't seem like they amount to much, imagine that the company has decided on a complete rebranding, or has just been acquired. What will the effort be to locate and change every trademark, logo, address, and slogan on every type of marketing literature, support document, user guide and other company documents?

What if the company needs everything to be provided in ten languages for the European market—how do you let the translators know the difference between company trade names, software commands, or product names and more general text in the documents? Someone will have to provide lists of words and phrases marked as "do not translate." If these are already marked as XML, it is simple to indicate that <tradename>, <command>, or <prodname> element content should not be translated.

Tagging existing document content as XML provides the means to extract it in meaningful ways for use in business processes.

Tagging for Import

The most basic way to create XML imports is to create placeholders in an InDesign template. The key issues are understanding where you want the XML to come in to the InDesign layout, how it should look, and what the structure of the incoming XML will be. For more information, see Chapter 3.

In business terms, you are creating an output in a nicely formatted, printable document form to meet a business need. You hand out a business card to assist in following up a sales lead, or you give someone a handy quick start guide for a newly purchased product. You provide a set of product specifications so that someone can decide if a product meets his or her needs. All of these are good reasons to use InDesign to deliver an aesthetically pleasing business document. It makes the most sense when you can take the leap to seeing InDesign as one delivery mechanism among many options (web page, phone solicitation, multimedia presentation) that can connect you to customers or suppliers or partners. Using the same content across various delivery formats is leveraging the content creation process to streamline processes and reduce errors.

Tagging for Iterative XML Development

InDesign only supports one type of XML content model (DTD), which doesn't differentiate numbers and dates as special types of data. So you can't easily control whether people are going to put text, numbers, or dates in a particular manner in your XML elements. In database terms, there isn't anything in InDesign that will enforce "data typing" in the XML that will be valid for doing calculations or other operations. If you accept this limitation, and generally view InDesign as a generator of text content, you will be fine with a database that expects text content in data fields.

If you really need to constrain the contents of an XML element to be a numeric value, a date/time or other data type than text, you will probably not be happy with InDesign's XML limitations in this regard. Within InDesign itself, the values of XML elements will be treated as text only. If someone types numbers, they are not truly numbers (integer or float) as far as any XML export is concerned.

XSLT would let you perform "casting" from the text values in elements to some other data type. As a post-export process, you could change text numbers into true numeric values, for example. Refer to O'Reilly's *XSLT Cookbook* by Sal Mangano for details.

Working Without an Initial DTD

For iterative development without a DTD, you look at the end result that you want, and the type of content that you are creating in InDesign, and design an output that will flow into the next process as simply as possible. This type of process works best for simple content that can be tagged in InDesign and mapped to a fairly shallow set of XML elements in the output.

Looking Forward: InDesign as an XML "Skin"

If you have a number of XML documents, all based on the same tags, you can make them look completely different just by using a different style mapping and page layout.

For example, say that in template *A.indt*, you have three columns, justified text, with Caslon Old Style as the base font. In template *B.indt*, you have a single-width column of left-aligned text with a narrow sidebar and Helvetica as the base font. In each template, you have mapped the XML tags to paragraph and character styles of the same name (but different definitions) and applied tags to text flows. By importing the XML of the same tag structure into the different InDesign templates, you will get completely different-looking documents.

The power of this technique is only beginning to be appreciated. It is held back by the fact that there is so little standardization of XML that people use in InDesign. I expect that the next development will be the introduction of XML standard tag sets (DTDs) for publications that are rich enough to describe information usefully, but not so deeply that they are difficult to use. Using standardized XML content models will provide the basis for increased automation with XSLT on import and export of XML.

If you want to explore this concept now, it is easy to try out:

1. Create an InDesign template (*.indt*) with styles, column layout, and so on that you like.

2. Use an XML file as the basis to create placeholder content with the tags you want to use. Map the tags to styles in the template.

3. Save a copy of the *.indt* file with a new name.

4. Open it and redefine the styles, change the column layout, and so on to make a different-looking design.

5. Import the XML into an InDesign file based on the first template. It should format itself with your styles.

6. Import the same XML, or other XML based on the same tags, into an InDesign file based on your second template. It should format itself with your other styles.

If you maintain the same set of XML tags and InDesign styles and the mappings between them, you can create as many different document looks as you care to design. As a designer, you can look at this process as similar to creating HTML skins for websites. You can commoditize the template design if you can get people to use the same XML tags for different content (or convert XHTML to XML using XSLT, as described in "Upcasting from HTML to XML for InDesign Import" (page 94)).

Exporting XML

Marking Up (Tagging) Existing Content for XML Export

The "tagging" process is generally quite straightforward. Select objects or text, and then click a tag name in the Tags window's list of tags (assuming that you have loaded tags). See the InDesign Help section "Tagging content to export to XML" for more information. For tables and images, I have provided more details in this section.

The Special Case of InDesign Tables (Namespaced XML)

A surprising number of layout people have never tried the table features of InDesign, preferring to group text frames to make tables. But because InDesign CS offers powerful table design and production, we will make good use of them for our XML processes.

We'll work through some table exercises. First, to understand how InDesign represents a table as XML, we will start by saving a tagged table as XML:

1. Select Table→Insert Table. The Insert Table dialog opens. Create this table as two columns, with one heading row and three normal rows.

2. Click in the top left edge of the first row to select the row, then select Table→Merge Cells to combine the two cells into a single row.

3. Repeat the Merge Cells operation for the second and fourth rows of the table, leaving the third row as two separate cells.

4. Now use Table→Select→Table to make sure the entire table is selected, then use the Tags palette to tag the entire table as `<CourseDescriptions>` (the root element of the sample XML file).

5. Select the top row and type COURSE DESCRIPTIONS as the heading for the entire table. Create a new paragraph style named TableHead1, making the text bold and large, and apply it to the top row of the table. Do not tag the top row as an XML element.

6. In the second row, type CourseDescription_Major. Apply the matching paragraph style, then select the row and tag it with the `<CourseDescription_Major>` XML tag name.

7. In the first cell of the third row, type "CourseDescription_Name". Apply the matching paragraph style, then select the cell (not the whole row), and tag it with the `<CourseDescription_Name>` XML tag name.

8. In the second cell of the third row, type "CourseDescription_Text". Apply the matching paragraph style, then select the cell (not the whole row), and tag it with the `<CourseDescription_Text>` XML tag name.

9. In the fourth row of the table, type "CourseDescription_Footnote". Apply the matching paragraph style, then select the row and tag it with the `<CourseDescription_Footnote>` XML tag name.

10. Below the table, type "Course offering subject to change. Check the website for current offerings." Create and apply a new paragraph style named Note that is a variation of the CourseDescription_Footnote paragraph style (smaller and in a different font so that it looks distinctive).

11. Save your file containing your styled and tagged table.

12. Select File→Save As Copy to freeze a copy of this file as a snapshot to which you can return.

Examining the Table

Open the Structure pane if it is not already open. If you watch the Structure pane while you move your cursor from place to place in the table, you will see a highlight on the element that has been used to tag each row or cell.

Notice that there is a new element in the Structure pane named Cell that contains the text for your table heading that you styled as TableHead1. The Tags palette (Figure 6-1) will now include new elements named `<Cell>` and `<Table>`.

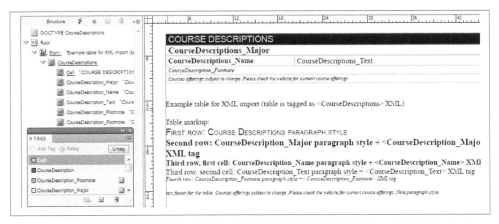

Figure 6-1. The Structure pane and Tags palette (left) and the table (right), showing that InDesign adds a new tag named Cell when untagged content is included in a tagged table

In CS5 and later versions
> When you use Edit→Edit in Story Editor, you will be able to see how each individual table cell is tagged with XML and what it contains.

In CS3 and CS4
> When you use Edit→Edit in Story Editor to look at your file, instead of seeing the angle symbols with XML element names around the text, you will only see the element names in the left panel (the Structure pane). InDesign CS3 and CS4 do not represent the tagged table content in the Story Editor view.

InDesign treats tables differently from all other XML. Tables are a specific type of object within the InDesign application that are different from text objects or media (image) objects. So InDesign has arbitrarily added new `<Table>` and `<Cell>` elements to your set of XML tags to accord with its internal representation of the table object.

Even more surprises await you when you export this test table as XML.

We'll perform two trials. For the first trial, select the entire text frame containing the table. While it is selected, select File→Export, then choose XML as the file type and name the file *placeholderTable01.xml*. Check the box to see the resulting XML in Internet Explorer. Leave the encoding as UTF-8 (the default). Click Export.

For the second trial, in the Structure pane, click in the `<CourseDescriptions>` element, then right-click to get a context menu. Select Export from Selected Item, and check the box to see the resulting XML in Internet Explorer. Type a different name for this file, such as *placeholderTable02.xml*. Leave the UTF-8 encoding, then click Export.

When you view the second file you made (*placeholderTable02.xml*) in Internet Explorer, you can see that it contains the XML elements within the `<CourseDescriptions>` element, including the `<Cell>` element that InDesign added to tag the first row.

In addition, you see a lot of XML markup that you did not explicitly apply. The top line now declares an XML namespace called `aid:` with this `xmlns` attribute (`xmlns:aid="http://ns.adobe.com/AdobeInDesign/4.0/"`) and adds to it some attributes (`aid:table`, `aid:trows`, and `aid:tcols`) of the `<CourseDescriptions>` element you used to tag the table. (For CS4 and CS5, the namespace `xmlns:aid5="http://ns.adobe.com/AdobeInDesign/5.0/"` is added to support table styles).

The root `<table>` element has a number of `aid:` attributes: `aid:table="table"`, `aid:trows="4"`, and `aid:tcols="2"`.

The header cells have markup for another set of `aid:` namespace attributes: `aid:theader=""`, `aid:crows="1"`, and `aid:ccols="2"`.

And the other cells also contain `aid:` namespace attributes, such as `aid:table="cell"`, `aid:crows="1"`, `aid:ccols="2"`, and `aid:ccolwidth="206.5010000000001"` (some long decimal value).

A complete example looks like this:

```
<CourseDescriptions xmlns:aid="http://ns.adobe.com/AdobeInDesign/4.0/"
 aid:table="table" aid:trows="4" aid:tcols="2">
  <Cell aid:table="cell" aid:theader="" aid:crows="1" aid:ccols="2">
      COURSE DESCRIPTIONS</Cell>
  <CourseDescription_Major aid:table="cell" aid:crows="1"
   aid:ccols="2">CourseDescriptions_Major</CourseDescription_Major>
  <CourseDescription_Name aid:table="cell" aid:crows="1" aid:ccols="1"
      aid:ccolwidth="206.5010000000001">CourseDescriptions_Name
  </CourseDescription_Name>
  <CourseDescription_Text aid:table="cell" aid:crows="1" aid:ccols="1"
      aid:ccolwidth="332.99900000000014">CourseDescriptions_Text
  </CourseDescription_Text>
  <CourseDescription_Footnote aid:table="cell" aid:crows="1"
   aid:ccols="2">CourseDescription_Footnote</CourseDescription_Footnote>
</CourseDescriptions>
```

The `aid:` namespace is used for many functions of InDesign under the hood. For now, it is important only that you see that the markup appears in the XML export even though you did not explicitly add it in InDesign.

Open the first table XML file you exported. You will see that this exported XML file contains the automatically generated Root and Story elements and, near the bottom, the untagged text you styled as a Note paragraph style:

```
<Root>
- <Story>
- <CourseDescriptions xmlns:aid="http://ns.adobe.com/AdobeInDesign/4.0/"
    aid:table="table" aid:trows="4" aid:tcols="2">
```

```
<Cell aid:table="cell" aid:theader="" aid:crows="1" aid:ccols="2">
    COURSE DESCRIPTIONS</Cell>
<CourseDescription_Major aid:table="cell" aid:theader="" aid:crows="1"
 aid:ccols="2">CourseDescriptions_Major</CourseDescription_Major>
<CourseDescription_Name aid:table="cell" aid:crows="1" aid:ccols="1"
    aid:ccolwidth="206.5010000000001">CourseDescriptions_Name
</CourseDescription_Name>
<CourseDescription_Text aid:table="cell" aid:crows="1" aid:ccols="1"
    aid:ccolwidth="332.99900000000014">CourseDescriptions_Text
</CourseDescription_Text>
<CourseDescription_Footnote aid:table="cell" aid:crows="1"
 aid:ccols="2">CourseDescription_Footnote</CourseDescription_Footnote>
</CourseDescriptions>

Course offerings subject to change. Please check the website for current course
offerings.

</Story>
</Root>
```

Notice that although the aid: namespace was added to <CourseDescriptions> and its child elements, it does *not* appear on the <Root> or <Story> elements or the untagged line of text.

From these two examples of exported XML, we can reverse engineer what will make InDesign "understand" and format imported XML as a table. The aid: namespace informs the program that we are using its underlying layout representation. To create a table upon import, we need to add the aid: namespace attributes to each XML element.

Interpreting the aid: attributes is fairly straightforward. The element that will become the table (generally some sort of wrapper element in the XML) minimally needs aid:table="table" and an aid:tcols attribute set to the value of the number of columns in the overall table layout, such as aid:tcols="4".

There is no <row> in InDesign tables. The value of aid:trows is optional for the element with the aid:table="table" attribute. If set, it may truncate imported XML at the specified number of rows. If left off, the rest of the imported content will determine the total number of rows in the table.

The values of the attributes aid:ccols and aid:crows govern the column and row spans, respectively, of an element with an attribute aid:table="cell". So, if on the table element the value is set with aid:tcols="2" and the cell-level element has the aid:ccols="2", then the cell-level element will span two columns, the width of the table. If aid:crows value is greater than 1, the cell will span the specified number of rows in the table.

Table 6-1 is a good reference to help you keep this behavior sorted out.

Table 6-1. Table attributes

Namespaced attribute name	Purpose
`aid:table`	Defines any table-related element.
`aid:table="table"`	Defines the table element itself.
`aid:tcols="N"`	Defines N number of columns in the table.
`aid:trows="N"`	Defines N number of rows in the table. You do not have to supply a value for this attribute, and you should omit it when importing XML to avoid having the XML truncated when it reaches the Nth value of `aid:trows`.
`aid:table="cell"`	Defines a cell within a table.
`aid:ccols="N"`	Defines N number of columns that the cell will span.
`aid:crows="N"`	Defines N number of rows that the cell will span.
`aid:theader=""`	Makes the cell a header, which enables it to be reused automatically at the top of every text frame for tables that flow from one text frame to another. This is always an attribute with an empty value " " because InDesign assumes that if it appears, it should be applied, so you don't have to type a "true" or false" for `aid:theader`.
`aid:tfooter=""`	Makes the cell a footer, which enables it to be repeated at the end of every text frame for tables that flow from one text frame to another. This is always an attribute with an empty value " " because InDesign assumes that if it appears, it should be applied, so you don't have to type a "true" or false" for `aid:tfooter`.
`aid:colwidth="NNN.nnnnn"`	Width of column (in points not pixels; approximately 72 points = 1 inch).
`aid5:tablestyle`	Starting with CS4, the ability to add a named table style to the table object. You need to have created a placeholder table with the named style in your InDesign template for the style to be applied automatically upon importing XML into InDesign.

You can find more information on `aid:` namespaces for tables in *Adobe InDesign CS3 and XML: A Technical Reference*, or search online for `aid:` or `aid5:` namespace)

Tables are tricky to work with, and if the namespace is confusing, the easiest way to create them is with the placeholder technique.

Tagging Images as XML in InDesign

Images are another special case in InDesign. Because a linked image is actually a separate file, InDesign needs a pointer to the linked image in a graphics frame in the document. So, you create a graphics frame, place a linked image into the frame (see the InDesign Help if you don't know how to do this), and tag it as an `<Image>` element. Then, you will need an attribute of the `<Image>` element named "href" and the path to the file folder and image file as its value, such as `<Image href="path/to/folder/myfine image.psd">`. Adobe has kindly provided some assistance; according to the InDesign

Help, "When you tag a graphics frame [with the Image tag], a reference to the graphic's location (on disk) is placed in the exported XML file." (If you use a different element name than <Image> to tag an image, the element is required to have the href attribute with the file path to the image file, the same as an <Image> element.)

Image Options in the Export XML Dialog

When you export XML that includes the tagged, linked images, InDesign provides a tab in the Export XML dialog with some choices. The Image Options are geared mostly to creating web-friendly image output. But you can simply copy the original images to a folder by checking the first checkbox, Original Images, below "Copy to Images Sub-Folder".

For the other two checkboxes, InDesign provides the same features: Image Conversion (Automatic, which decides the file format based on image content, or GIF or JPEG for all images), and settings for color palette and image quality and the like. See Figure 6-2.

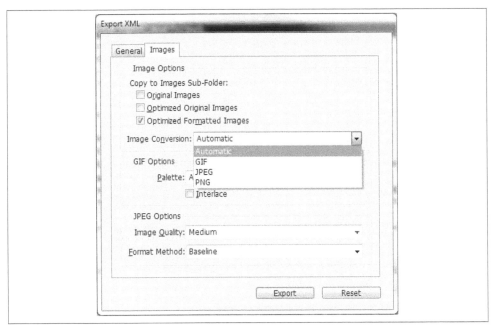

Figure 6-2. The Export XML dialog's Images tab, which provides optimization for web images

If you choose to optimize images (formatted or not), the XML output includes special attributes that point to the subfolder (automatically named *images*) and also to the location of the original image. In this example, `<Image href_fmt="images/01_f_fmt.jpg" href="file:///C:/adobeTutorial/ID_XML_Tutorial/Links/01_f.psd"/>` the `href_fmt` attribute contains the relative path to the optimized image from the current InDesign document. The `href` attribute points to a local file folder location of the original image that was placed in the document.

If you choose to copy original images to the subfolder, then your *.psd*, *.ai*, or other format image files would simply be duplicated in the *images* folder.

 You can use XSLT to change InDesign's `<Image>` elements into a different element, such as the HTML `<img>`, and just copy the `href` onto it. Or you can write a different `href` value (path to a server folder). If you want to do this, I recommend testing it first as a post-export transformation, rather than as "Apply XSLT on Export" (which is more likely to crash).

Exporting ePub Content (InDesign CS5.5 and CS6)

Export in XML Order Compared with Page Layout and Article Pane Order

Since InDesign CS5.5, there have been three methods to determine the content sequence when exporting ePubs from InDesign files: "Based on Page Layout", "Same as XML Structure", and "Same as Articles Panel" (see Figure 7-1).

The effects of the setting for Content Order are the same as for HTML exports:

Based on Page Layout
> This setting follows left–right and top–bottom order in general (based on page geometry); however, any unanchored text frame or graphics frame will move to the end of the output.

Same as XML Structure
> This setting will export *only* the content that has been tagged as XML, in the order in which it is seen in the Structure view. An image that is tagged but is not anchored can be located between other XML elements, and it will be exported in the location where it is seen in the Structure pane. However, there are some very odd behaviors when exporting ePub in XML order if you use alternate layouts with XML in the InDesign file. See the following section, "Alternate Layouts and XML Are Not Compatible Features" (page 58).

Same as Articles Panel

This setting will export *only* the content that is placed into articles. Unanchored text or graphic frames will be moved to the end of the output; it isn't possible to insert them in the middle of a text flow without anchoring them. When they are anchored, they will come out in the article where they are anchored.

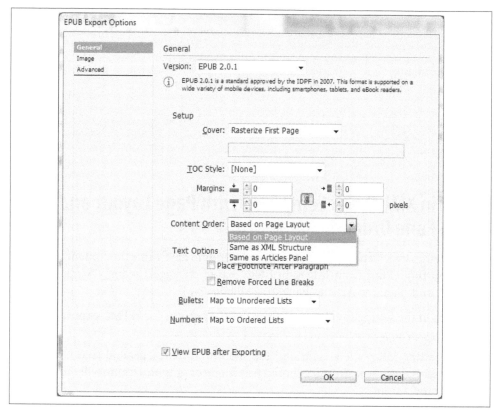

Figure 7-1. The EPUB Export Options dialog General tab, showing the Content Order dropdown

Alternate Layouts and XML Are Not Compatible Features

Adobe introduced alternate layouts to help people create content for iPad, Nook, and other digital readers. There are several problems with using alternate layouts when you have XML in the Structure pane:

- If you make an alternate layout, the intention is that you can link the text flows when they are reused in the different layout. So if you edit the text in the master layout, you can then update the linked text in the alternated layout pages and the text will be synchronized in the alternate layout without having to copy and paste the changes. That approach works well except that if you have XML tags applied to the text, when you make an alternate layout, the XML structure is duplicated in the Structure pane. If you export the XML after making the alternate layout, you will see the duplicated content.

- If you don't pay attention when you are editing the XML, you might make a change in the tags in the duplicate XML instead of the master. If you do this, the tags will not be replicated in the master layout's Structure pane. The linking between the text frames of the alternate layout and the master layout is one-way from the master to the alternate.

- If you use Epub Export Options→Content Order→Same as XML Structure, there seem to be bugs in what happens with XML tagged after you create the alternate layout. Sometimes it appears that InDesign doesn't "see" an unanchored image that is added to the XML by tagging it. If you force a refresh of the ePub export, for example by turning on the checkbox to remove manual line breaks, then the un-anchored image may show up in the ePub.

Because the relationships between the text frames in alternate layouts and the XML do not seem to have been considered by Adobe, you may want to select and untag the text frames that are in your alternate layouts and leave XML tags only in the master layout. This approach will prevent duplicate XML structures and reduce the chance that you will make XML edits in the wrong layout.

Exporting an InDesign CS6 file containing alternate layouts as an ePub in XML order is not a supported feature of InDesign. Even without XML in a layout, there appears to be a fundamental problem in the ePub export process from InDesign files containing alternate layouts at the time of this writing. Alternate layouts were created for PDF and SWF export, not for ePub.

Go here (*http://indesignsecrets.com/printing-and-exporting-alternate-layouts.php*) for a discussion of problems in using alternate layouts and exporting ePub or HTML.

Untested: Liquid Layout and InDesign Files Containing XML Structure

The Liquid Layout feature set was introduced in InDesign CS6 to help designers create content that can dynamically resize when viewed on different devices. Go here (*https://www.adobe.com/products/indesign/features.html*) for the feature overview and links to more details on Liquid Layout. As Liquid Layout affects only positioning of objects on pages, there is probably no impact to the XML structure. But this feature was not tested for this edition of this book.

Validating XML in InDesign

A foolish consistency is the hobgoblin of little minds.

—Ralph Waldo Emerson

Why Validate?

Validation is the process of assuring that the XML you create conforms to the rules of your structure, whether governed by a DTD, schema, or database structure. Although "a foolish consistency" in philosophy may not be praiseworthy, a wise consistency in content creation may save you a lot of later effort.

When you validate your XML content, the assumption is that any other system using the same structural rules can use the XML you create. For solo content creators who are only making XML and storing it for their own uses, validation may not be necessary. But for anyone who is working with XML with the intent of passing along the content they create to other applications or processes, making sure that the XML is valid will be imperative.

How to Validate XML in InDesign

Adobe has given you the ability to make mistakes when creating XML content, then go back and fix them by checking the content's validity against a DTD. If you need really robust validation while authoring XML content, InDesign is not the right choice for your publishing needs. Adobe FrameMaker and other XML publishing applications that offer a guided content creation process (preventing you from inserting invalid structure in your document) will serve you better.

Consider InDesign as a tool for which validation should be done *before* importing XML (if possible) or frequently while creating XML structure within an InDesign document.

To use InDesign's validation features, you must first load a DTD. If your organization is using XML elsewhere, you may have been provided a DTD that you can use for creating XML in InDesign. If not, you may want to consider what type of DTDs already in existence would serve your needs.

Useful XML rulesets that can be found online include DITA (for topic-based content that is suitable to repurpose as online help), NewsML (for news articles), and NLM (for journal articles and scientific papers). Most DTDs have low-level structures (titles, sub-heads, tables, lists, links, images, and generic paragraphs) that will be very similar to HTML tags. More complex DTDs also provide "semantic" tags that help you understand the meaning of a piece of content, such as bylines, author names, product specifications, units of measure, mathematical equations, chemical structures, and so on. I recommend using the simplest DTD you can find (or create) that will provide the minimum structure you need.

You should work locally with a copy of the DTD, rather than pointing to a DTD on a server on the Internet. Save the DTD on your own computer in the folder with the InDesign documents or in a common server that a group of content creators can access. Just remember two things: you should use the markup in the way that the DTD was intended (not by guessing, but by having documentation that explains how it is to be used), and you should *never* alter a DTD yourself if it is being used by a group of people.

Complex DTDs may consist of multiple *.dtd*, *.mod*, and *.ent* files that combine to provide the complete XML content model. You may have to create a single DTD file from these files that includes all the elements that you expect to use in the content and removes ones that you never plan to use. An example is making a subset DTD of DocBook that removes all the software and user interface elements if you are not making a software handbook.

The complexity of a deep DTD will make it very hard to select and use the correct element from the InDesign Tag menu. There are limited methods to assist with this problem: you can use the methods of creating a simpler XML described in Chapter 11 or use scripting at the SDK level to create dialogs for applying styles that are much more context-aware than the "Map Style to Tags" feature.

If you link the XML files that you place in InDesign, you can use the Links panel to open the linked XML file in an external XML editor, if you have one installed. This allows you to edit and validate the file with a better tool, and provides context-sensitive XML authoring that InDesign lacks. You will have to apply styles to edited or new content when you return to InDesign.

Loading a DTD and Getting the Correct Root Element

To add a DTD to your InDesign document, open the Structure pane, click on the upper-right-corner arrow icon to get the Structure menu, then select Load DTD. Browse to where the DTD is located and select it. If you do this in an empty InDesign document, you will automatically get a root element tagged with the default <Root> element that InDesign provides. InDesign will load all of the tags from the DTD in alphabetical order into the Tags palette when you load the DTD. To apply the root element from your own XML tags, open the Tags palette, select the default <Root> element, and retag it with the real root element of your DTD.

Authoring with a DTD

After you have loaded the DTD and applied the correct tag to the root element, you can start authoring and validating as you go. Example 8-1 contains an example DTD.

Example 8-1. A simple DTD for course descriptions

```
<?xml version="1.0" encoding="UTF-8"?>
<!--DTD generated by XML Spy v4.3 U (http://www.xmlspy.com)-->
<!ELEMENT CourseDescriptions (CourseDescription_Major | CourseDescription)+>
<!ELEMENT CourseDescription_Major (#PCDATA)>
<!ELEMENT CourseDescription (CourseDescription_Name | CourseDescription_Text |
    CourseDescription_Footnote)+>
<!ELEMENT CourseDescription_Name (#PCDATA)>
<!ELEMENT CourseDescription_Text (#PCDATA)>
<!ELEMENT CourseDescription_Footnote (#PCDATA)>
<!ATTLIST CourseDescription_Footnote
    type CDATA #REQUIRED>
```

This DTD[1] states that I have a root element <CourseDescriptions> that can contain multiple <CourseDescription_Major> and <CourseDescription> elements. There aren't any structures inside a <CourseDescription_Major>, only text (PCDATA).

Within a <CourseDescription>, there are <CourseDescription_Name>, <CourseDescription_Text>, and <CourseDescription_Footnote> elements. These elements don't contain any other element structures.

<CourseDescription_Footnote> has a required attribute of type (used mainly to indicate when there is a prerequisite for the course mentioned in the footnote).

---

1. This is an extremely simple DTD. I will not go into detail about how to read DTDs and how to write them, but I suggest that you read up on them online or in a book such as *XML Elements of Style* by Simon St. Laurent (McGraw-Hill, 1999).

Create a text frame and tag it with the root element of your DTD by dragging the root element onto the text frame (use the text selection tool when dragging). To see if the tag has been applied, select View→Structure→Show Tagged Frames.

With the text cursor in the tagged text frame, select the square New Element icon in the top bar of the Structure pane. In the dialog that opens (see Figure 8-1), select the next Tag that you need from the drop-down list (this list can be very long for a complex DTD), and it will be added to the structure, indented below the root element.

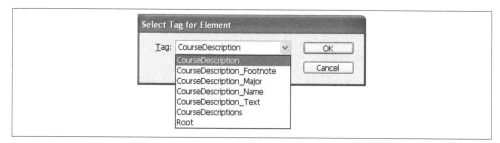

Figure 8-1. Adding an element with the Structure pane icon (by selecting a tag name from the drop-down list)

You can test whether you've added the first element that the DTD requires by clicking the Validation icon (the lightning bolt in the top bar of the Structure pane). A subwindow appears at the bottom of the Structure pane and will display the words "no known errors" if you selected the correct element to add below your root element.

Dealing with Validation Problems

If you see that the element you inserted has turned red when you click the Validation icon, the validation window will display an error message and suggestions for how to fix the structure. If you click on the suggestion that you think will solve the validation problem, the suggested fix will be applied in the Structure pane. If it is correct according to the DTD, the element will no longer be red in the structure pane.

One problem with the suggestions that InDesign makes is that many of them are not helpful to the process of creating content quickly. For example, if I insert a `<CourseDescription>` element inside a `<CourseDescription_Major>` element, InDesign states that the element is not valid in that position in the structure and suggests that I delete the element (Figure 8-2).

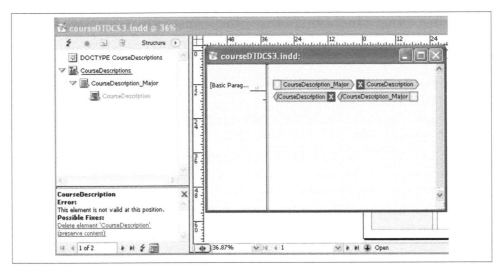

Figure 8-2. InDesign's suggested solution for an element in the wrong place

Although this action will fix my problem, it is not the best solution. The DTD requires that the `<CourseDescription>` element be at the same level of indentation as the `<CourseDescription_Major>` (a "sibling" element, rather than a "child"). It would be better for me to move the `<CourseDescription>` element out of and below the `<Cour seDescription_Major>` element, as my intention was to add a `<CourseDescription>` to the structure. To move an element, select it in the Structure pane, and drag it to the new location (the location where it will be dropped into the structure is indicated by a bold line).

If I validate the structure now, the `<CourseDescription>` element turns red and multiple suggestions are displayed in the validation window. InDesign recognizes that the `<CourseDescription>` element must contain other elements (for the name, descriptive text and footnotes) to be valid.

 Use Edit→View in Story Editor to see the element tags more clearly when you are not typing text within the elements. You can also add line breaks and rearrange (drag) elements in Story Editor View.

Why Authoring XML with a DTD is Problematic in InDesign

1. It is easy to accidentally retag the root element in the Structure pane with an invalid element name.

2. Multiple suggestions may display in the validation window, so to select the correct one, you must understand the DTD in depth.

3. InDesign cannot move elements to the correct locations in a structure for you, so it will suggest that you delete elements that are inserted in the wrong location. In practice, you will usually want to drag the element to a different location.

4. The Structure pane drag-and-drop action can be tricky to do correctly on long documents.

I can click each of the suggestions to insert the missing elements (Figure 8-3). InDesign will add them to the Structure in the order that I click the suggestions. Or, I can use the Add Element icon to insert the three subelements inside the <CourseDescription> element. I just select <CourseDescription> in the Structure pane, and then add the other elements one by one in the order that I want them to appear.

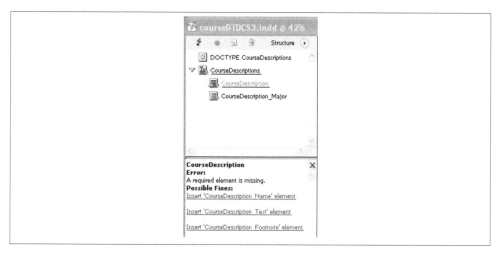

Figure 8-3. Multiple suggested fixes in the validation window (lower left)

When I validate, this time the <CourseDescription_Major> and <CourseDescrip tion> are not red, so the problem has been fixed. However, the <CourseDescrip tion_Footnote> I added is red, and the validation window suggests that I add the required type attribute (Figure 8-4)

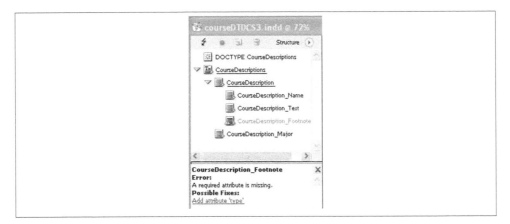

Figure 8-4. A validation error and suggestion for a missing attribute

When I click the suggestion, an empty attribute named `type` is added to the `<Course Description_Footnote>`. When I click the Validation icon, the structure is now valid, even though I have not supplied any value for the `type` attribute.

If I double-click the `type` attribute, the Add Attribute dialog opens, and I can type in the value for this attribute, such as "prerequisite." I need to know what the choices are for the value of the attribute—for instance, if they are constrained, or whether I can put in any value I want (in this case, I can). So again, it is important to understand how your DTD works in detail to author valid XML in InDesign.

Occurrence and Sequences of Elements

Many DTDs limit the occurrence and sequence of elements at different places in the structure they define. A constraint that allows only one element of a given kind, or a sequence of elements in a certain order, may determine how you author XML in InDesign. Such constraints add to the complexity of the validation process.

 Validate early and often when working with XML and DTDs for the first time. Once you have created a set of valid structures, you can write a procedure to follow so that your next XML document authoring session will be less difficult.

In the case of my DTD, the `<CourseDescription_Major>` and `<CourseDescription>` element can occur multiple times, and the sequence is not constrained. So I can have a `<CourseDescription>` element before a `<CourseDescription_Major>` element, even though that is probably not what I really want. But I will resist the temptation to "improve" the DTD by adding more constraints to the structure model. Logically, any

`<CourseDescription>` might be a child of a `<CourseDescription_Major>`, but there might be courses that are not associated with a major. The database model that was the origin of the elements for this DTD is not constrained in this regard, and I want to maintain synchronization with that database.

InDesign has enough DTD awareness to provide some XML editing choices based on a DTD, such as inserting a parent element to wrap a selected element or inserting an element or adding an attribute into the cursor location in the Structure pane. The entire list of XML elements in the DTD will be displayed in a drop-down menu for you to choose the element, but it is up to you to know which element is valid or best to use. If you select an element as a wrapper or insert a new element or attribute, you should validate it immediately afterward, before you move on to another activity.

 Schemas (not DTDs) based on database tables can be generated from many database applications. InDesign does not support schemas, so you will need to use another XML tool to convert the schema to a DTD to use in InDesign.

Validating Outside of InDesign

As a reality check when working with a DTD, even when InDesign reports "no known errors," you can double-check the XML's validity. Export the XML with the choice to Include DTD Declaration checked in the Export XML Options dialog (Figure 8-5).

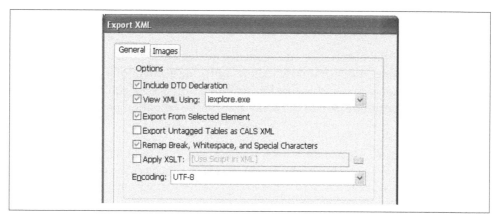

Figure 8-5. Export the DTD declaration in the XML output for external validation

Now the XML can be tested in another XML application that has validation capabilities. In XML Spy, the exported file opens without any warnings if the file is valid. Here is what my valid sample (empty) XML elements look like:

```
<?xml version="1.0" encoding="UTF-8" standalone="no"?>
<!DOCTYPE CourseDescriptions SYSTEM "C:\Textenergy\oreillybooks\shortCut\
    coursedescriptions.dtd">
<CourseDescriptions>
    <CourseDescription>
        <CourseDescription_Name/>
        <CourseDescription_Text/>
        <CourseDescription_Footnote type="whatever"/>
    </CourseDescription>
    <CourseDescription_Major/>
</CourseDescriptions>
```

There are many other things that you should know about working with DTDs, schemas, databases, and creating valid XML. Consider acquiring a book or researching these subjects online if you plan to become proficient in XML.

Duplicating Structure to Build XML

Once you have a block of elements that is valid, you can duplicate the structure to build your XML document more rapidly. Select an element structure that you want to copy in the Structure pane. Then use Copy to put it on the clipboard. Select the copied element structure's *parent* element and paste it. The duplicate structure will be added to the end of the current structure of the parent element.

 Paste operations add content to the end of the parent structure. In In-Design, you can't paste an element structure between other elements that are siblings. If you want an element or structure to be placed in between existing sibling structures, you have to drag the new XML content after you paste it.

Duplicating is much faster than tagging plain text paragraphs with XML elements after you type the text. When you have created blocks of duplicate structures with copy/paste, you can switch to the Story Editor and start typing text into the elements.

 Don't forget to switch back to the Layout view to see how your line breaks, spaces, and tabs look on the page. Although the Story Editor is great for seeing the start and end tags of your elements, it is easy to forget to insert breaks and have XML elements that run together on the page.

Cleaning Up Imported XML Content

You should run the validation on any XML that you import into InDesign for which you have a DTD. With a large XML file, this step can be problematic, because you will have a large number of suggestions in the validation window to work through. If possible, validate the XML *before* importing it into InDesign.

Fast and Light Credo: Develop Now, Validate Later

If there is no DTD available for you, you can create one from sample XML yourself. Start by making a list of the different information bits that will make up your content structure. For example, suppose that I am trying to get some personnel information into my course catalog. When looking at the text in the current unstructured document, I see that there are people who have administrative positions, people who are on various boards, people who have won awards, people who are on staff, and various types of teachers on the faculty. All of these people are employees, except some of the board members. All of the faculty have their degrees, degree-granting institutions, and any special awards listed after their names. In another part of the catalog, these people are listed with phone numbers.

I can choose `<personnel>` as my root element (despite knowing that a few people are technically not employees). Then I can have a `<person>` with `<name>` elements patterned on a standard model such as `<lastname>` `<firstname>` `<mi>` and `<honorific>`. Each person can also have contact information (`<phone>`, `<email>`, etc.) and `<degrees>` containing `<degree>` and `<institution>` elements.

With this as a starting point, I can model the XML directly in InDesign. I work in much the same way that I did when I was using a DTD, except that I don't validate as I go. Once I have a good example set of XML elements, I export the XML. Then with another XML tool, such as XML Spy or Oxygen, I generate a DTD based on the sample.

Once I have an initial DTD, I load it into my InDesign document that contains the sample XML content and validate the XML with it. Assuming that it validates, I continue to make XML to match the structure model of my DTD.

Iterating the Information Structure and DTD

At some point in my development, someone may ask for a new element in the XML structure. Perhaps he or she wants to add the teacher's department to each person who is a teacher and an office location to each staff and administrative person. I can add this new element structure based on some database fields used for the college's online directory or by looking at a printed directory to see what headings and information are in the directory that describe the locations of people on campus (such as the building name and/or number, the floor, room or suite, etc.).

I now delete the current DTD from the Structure pane in InDesign because I don't want a lot of validation errors with my new structure. I add the <location> elements to the contact information for each person in a three-phase process:

1. I build a placeholder for the <location> structure with all the new elements I want in the first <person> element of my XML content. I export the XML again so that the new <location> structure is included in the sample XML that I use for DTD development.

2. I regenerate a DTD with my other XML tool, then load it into my InDesign document and validate the XML that contains my new structure. If I have made the new <location> structure *required*, every <person> element that is missing the <location> structure will now generate an error in the validation window.

3. I repair the XML so that it will validate with the revised DTD. I can duplicate the first <location> structure by selecting it in the Structure pane and doing a copy/paste operation to add it to the other <person> element structures. Then I can validate again and continue fixing the structure until I see the "no known errors" message in the validation window.

 If you know how to work with XSLT, this would be faster than manually adding elements with a copy/paste operation. You can write a template that adds new XML structures to your existing XML file. Consult books such as *XSLT Cookbook* by Sal Mangano (O'Reilly, 2002) or online references on XSLT for more information on adding structures or modifying existing ones.

The process of creating the new structure, generating a revised DTD, and validating can be repeated as I make changes to the structure. At each iteration, I can demonstrate the XML to stakeholders to see if it meets their needs. Once everyone has agreed to a structure, I can annotate the final DTD with comments so that everyone knows what each element is and how many times it can occur and in what sequence. This documentation then gets distributed to anyone else who needs to create XML or use the XML that is being created.

Despite all your best efforts to document how the DTD should be used, and to train authors, someone will always create invalid XML content in InDesign. InDesign does not provide enough XML authoring support in its current incarnation. If the content authors are struggling, you might investigate other XML authoring tools that help authors use a DTD. Adobe makes another product, FrameMaker, which provides guided authoring for XML based on a DTD. FrameMaker costs about the same as InDesign but requires more expert assistance to set up for XML import and export than does InDesign. A number of other XML editors and authoring tools (freeware, shareware, or commercial) are also available that may meet your authoring needs and budget.

If you use an XML authoring tool other than FrameMaker or InDesign itself, you can still import the XML you create into InDesign to make a visually pleasing document. In this regard, InDesign provides sufficient functionality to be very useful for XML publishing. Validate the XML before you import it. Then use the techniques described in this book to map to paragraph and character styles.

What InDesign Cannot Do
(or Do Well) with XML

It's fairly natural to expect that you could use one piece of XML data in multiple places in an InDesign layout—but that's not at all the way that InDesign works. Once you've imported XML, there is a one-to-one correspondence between the elements in the Structure view and their expression in the layout. If you want an element to appear multiple times, you've got to duplicate the element for each appearance on a document page. (Obviously, you can get around this in some cases by placing the XML element on a master page.)

—Olav Martin Kvern and David Blatner,
Real World Adobe InDesign CS4

The 1:1 Import Conundrum

As the epigraph to this chapter states (and this is still true for InDesign versions up to CS5), the expectation is that you import one XML file to fill one content area (text flow) in your InDesign document. This requirement is contradictory to the spirit of XML, which is all about reuse of content in multiple documents and in multiple ways. For example, you might want a standard warning or copyright or other block of content to appear in many places in a single document of a set of documents collected as a book. However, from the Structure pane, you cannot drag the same piece of structure into multiple locations in an InDesign document. If you drag an element into the layout a second time, InDesign will remove it from its first location in the layout.

Bad Characters

Some typographic controls may generate characters—even in later versions of InDesign—that are not XML-compatible. Adobe mentions this in the InDesign Help section about exporting XML: "Not all characters are supported in XML (such as the Automatic Page Number character). InDesign warns you if it cannot include a character in the XML file."

CS2 only

> InDesign CS2 XML export controls are more limited than those in InDesign CS3 and later. CS2 does not have the Remap Break, Whitespace, and Special Characters option. As a consequence, the XML that you generate from InDesign CS2 may contain characters used in publishing applications that are problematic in XML processing. Chief of these are the characters that make paragraph and manual line breaks in the text layout. XML doesn't use these types of characters, and depending on the processes you run after exporting XML from InDesign, you may have to clean up the XML to remove these types of characters. See Figure 9-1.

Figure 9-1. Unwanted characters (square) in XML exported from InDesign CS2

All versions of InDesign CS

> Related to the "bad characters" export problem is the issue of imported XML that might contain tabs, spaces, and line breaks. Often this problem is seen in applications that "pretty print" XML files with indents and coloring to make them easier to read. For example, I use SynchroSoft Oxygen Editor. When the pretty-printed XML created in Oxygen is used for import, it creates unwanted effects in the layout.
>
> To get a clean import, it is sometimes necessary to edit the text in a text editor to remove the tabs and spaces, play with the import dialog whitespace controls (do not import contents of whitespace-only elements in CS3 and later), or run an XSL transformation to remove line endings and tabs from the XML before importing it into InDesign.

Inscrutable Errors, Messages, and Crashes

InDesign often provides helpful error notifications, messages, and crash information—and sometimes not-so-helpful versions of these, such as the following:

Devilish validation suggestions

Are you missing a required attribute? Have you forgotten to put a required element in your structure? The validation window at the bottom of the structure pane will tell you the sad story of your incompetence with the DTD, but the suggestions it offers won't always tell you enough about fixing the problem—see Chapter 8 for more information.

Exporting from the element with the included DTD will not be valid

Several times when I had a DTD included in the XML that I was exporting and checked the box to include the DTD declaration on export, I saw a message that the XML I was exporting was not going to be valid using the DTD. It seemed to me at the time that the message was bogus, as I had validated the content with the DTD before export. I opened the exported content in XML Spy to check it, and found that there was some kind of invisible (line break) character in the XML between elements. When I switched to EditPlus and looked at the same file, I saw square box characters in these places in the XML file. I had to do a search and replace on that character to get an XML file that would validate. This problem is related to the issue described in "Bad Characters" (page 74).

Making InDesign "think" too hard on import or export with XSL

It seemed to me that I was most likely to cause InDesign to crash if I tried to get too fancy with my XSLT. I am accustomed to being able to sort, filter, wrap, and unwrap elements; make substring operations on text in elements; and other tricks of the XSL trade. If I used these types of functions in XSLT that I was using when importing or exporting XML with InDesign, sometimes it didn't work, and sometimes it froze the application. See Chapter 10. My recommendation, if you need to do a lot of fancy manipulation of your XML, is to use XSLT as a pre- or postprocessing step external to InDesign.

InDesign Is Not an XML Authoring Tool

The premise of Adobe's XML tools for InDesign is that people with databases often have XML content that can be mapped to InDesign paragraph and character styles or to tables and images. There is no mapping to "container" elements that are used in making deeply nested XML structures. This behavior has implications for XML developers, but even more so for InDesigners who have to work with XML inside InDesign, as I wrote in my LinkedIn group, "XML Content/InDesign Publishing"—see the sidebar "Deep Structures and Flat Apps: The Contradictions of XML and InDesign for Designers" (page 76).

Deep Structures and Flat Apps: The Contradictions of XML and InDesign for Designers

By its nature, XML has hierarchy which leads to "deep" structures of elements within elements within elements . . . to the limits of the content model (DTD or schema). By nature, the design applications are only managing the styling or visual presentation of the content, and there is minimal "structure." In InDesign, the "structure" is: file, layout spread, page template, text frame, graphic frame, styles (object, table, paragraph, character), link (image or other linked resource), fonts, color swatches, etc. Did you notice that there is *no* subdivision of the text other than paragraph or character styles? Unlike a web page, which at least lets you arbitrarily group content into "div" container elements, there is no grouping or containing mechanism for text in InDesign besides the text frame.

This results in technical difficulties not just in placing deeply structured content into InDesign, which is mapping complexity to simplicity. It makes it even more troublesome to reverse the operation, by trying to restore a deep structure from a simple structure. Reconstructing XML from styles and the text of paragraphs or characters has to rely on a degree of consistency in the InDesign file that is hard for the layout person to maintain.

A more subtle problem is the cognitive shift that is required to get people who work with layout and styles to understand what hierarchical content is (and why hierarchy is useful). A person who has worked with visual design professionally is not necessarily going to immediately understand what the purpose of XML is. Instead, she is going to get caught up in the technical difficulty—and XML is likely to make her have to deal with obscure problems and unfamiliar menus in InDesign that have nothing to do with her primary job function of making beautiful pages. This results in frustration and resistance to adopting XML. And that attitude is *not* the designer's fault. It is arising directly from the tension between the worlds of structured content and flat presentations.

If, despite the difficulties, you must work with XML and keep it valid, the topics in Chapter 8 explains some of the challenges you will face.

Advanced Topics: Transforming XML with XSL

Topics in this section deal with transforming XML during import and export using the eXtensible Stylesheet Language Transforms (XSLT). Anyone can write XSLT with a text editor. Refer to Appendix A for some useful books to learn more about XSLT.

An aside regarding scripting InDesign and XML rules-based publishing

There is a lot of potential hidden in the phrase "XML Scripting," available since InDesign CS3. The power tools are scripting (AppleScript, Visual Basic and JavaScript) and rules-based XML publishing.

Scripting InDesign is a developer's delight—for developers who like print publishing. If you want to get a better idea of what can be done, see the O'Reilly Short Cut publications, such as *Scripting InDesign with JavaScript* by Peter Kahrel (O'Reilly, 2006). (Despite the original date of the book, the scripting reference is still valid.)

You can get started with the scripts by visiting the Adobe website (*http://www.adobe.com*) and searching for "scripting reference" documentation in the InDesign Help and Forum sections of the site. Online searches will reveal more InDesign scripting references.

XSLT for Wrangling XML versus XML Scripting for Automating XML Publishing

Here's what I think are the key differentiators for which process to use and why: if you need to change the XML structure itself as it is being imported or exported into InDesign, use XSL transforms. I provide some examples later in this book. InDesign has its limitations in transforming XML on import and export; the trick is to know when to "speak InDesign" and how.

 Although I provide working examples that you can copy, I do not detail every step that I take in writing the XSLT.

If you need to use InDesign to handle tasks that are inherent to InDesign itself, such as Map Tags to Styles, you could use the XML scripting capabilities. Figure 10-1 lists some of the available scripts.

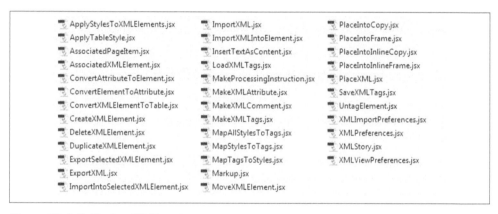

ApplyStylesToXMLElements.jsx	ImportXML.jsx	PlaceIntoCopy.jsx
ApplyTableStyle.jsx	ImportXMLIntoElement.jsx	PlaceIntoFrame.jsx
AssociatedPageItem.jsx	InsertTextAsContent.jsx	PlaceIntoInlineCopy.jsx
AssociatedXMLElement.jsx	LoadXMLTags.jsx	PlaceIntoInlineFrame.jsx
ConvertAttributeToElement.jsx	MakeProcessingInstruction.jsx	PlaceXML.jsx
ConvertElementToAttribute.jsx	MakeXMLAttribute.jsx	SaveXMLTags.jsx
ConvertXMLElementToTable.jsx	MakeXMLComment.jsx	UntagElement.jsx
CreateXMLElement.jsx	MakeXMLTags.jsx	XMLImportPreferences.jsx
DeleteXMLElement.jsx	MapAllStylesToTags.jsx	XMLPreferences.jsx
DuplicateXMLElement.jsx	MapStylesToTags.jsx	XMLStory.jsx
ExportSelectedXMLElement.jsx	MapTagsToStyles.jsx	XMLViewPreferences.jsx
ExportXML.jsx	Markup.jsx	
ImportIntoSelectedXMLElement.jsx	MoveXMLElement.jsx	

Figure 10-1. InDesign XML scripts

If you want to try more advanced automation, there are scripts for what Adobe terms "rules-based XML publishing" (Figure 10-2).

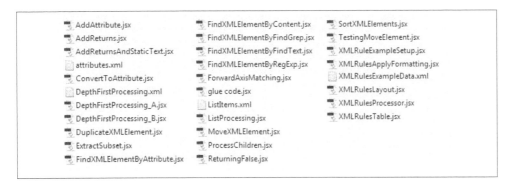

Figure 10-2. InDesign XML rules scripts

The rules are intended for the high-end publishing workflows used by magazine, catalog, and newspaper publishers. They are not shipped with the regular distribution of scripts in the InDesign Scripts folder. You may have to contact someone via the forums (*http://forums.adobe.com/community/indesign/indesign_scripting*) to get these scripts now.

It's beyond the scope of a small book such as this to explore scripting and XML rules. Take a look at books such as Grant Gamble's *InDesign CS5 Automation Using XML & JavaScript* or Shirley W. Hopkins's *AppleScripting Adobe InDesign CS5 and CS5.5* (both published through Createspace, 2011).

Now, on to what you might want to do with XML in InDesign using XSLT.

XSL: Extracting Elements from a Source XML File for a New Use

Sometimes, you know that there is content inside the main XML document that you would like to use for another purpose. The most common alternative purpose is something like making a list of figures or a table of contents from captions and titles in the XML file. But you can be more creative. Perhaps you need to find all of the keywords that were tagged in an XML file and extract them to build the foundations for a glossary XML file. Here is some XML content with keywords:

```
<Story name="Residency Requirements">
   <SectionHead>Residency Requirements</SectionHead>
   <para>New York State law requires that all students  file proof of
         residence each academic year. For New York State residents,
         the proper form should be submitted upon registration.
         Until you comply with this requirement, you will be billed the
         <keyword>non-resident tuition rate</keyword> (twice the resident
         rate).
   </para>
   <topic title="Residents of Monroe County">
       <SubHeads>Residents of Monroe County</SubHeads>
```

```
        <para>If you have been a permanent legal resident of New York State
            for the past year, and a resident of Monroe County for the
            last six months,complete a Residency Certificate
            <keyword>Affidavit</keyword>, sign it, and submit it
            with your registration.
        </para>
    </topic> ...
</Story>
```

An XSL transform can be pretty simple:

```
<xsl:stylesheet version="1.0" xmlns:xsl="http://www.w3.org/1999/XSL/Transform">
    <xsl:output method="xml" version="1.0" encoding="UTF-8" indent="no"/>
    <xsl:template match="/">
        <!-- make a new root element for the glossary XML -->
        <xsl:element name="glossary">
            <xsl:for-each select="//keyword">
                <!-- make an element for the term -->
                <xsl:element name="term">Term: <xsl:value-of select="."/>
                </xsl:element>
                <!-- make an element for the definition -->
                <xsl:element name="definition">Definition: </xsl:element>
            </xsl:for-each>
        </xsl:element>
    </xsl:template>
</xsl:stylesheet>
```

The results will be very useful: a new glossary XML file, with keywords as terms, and a blank definition element following each term, ready for an author to work on. Because the keywords were in the source XML and they are all now terms in the output XML, the transform makes it easy to correlate the glossary to the document that contains the keywords by filling in the definition:

```
<?xml version="1.0" encoding="UTF-8"?>
<glossary>
    <term>Term: non-resident tuition rate</term>
    <definition>Definition: </definition>
    <term>Term: Affidavit</term>
    <definition>Definition: </definition>
</glossary>
```

This type of XSL seems to work well on an existing InDesign file tagged with keywords. Upon export, if the XSL is used, the resulting file will just be the glossary XML, which you can put in a document of its own or into sidebars in a separate text flow in the same document as the original XML.

Alternatively, you could export the entire document XML and then apply the transform to the exported XML (using an XSLT processor such as Oxygen or XMLSpy) to get your starting glossary XML file.

XSL: Getting the Elements to Sort Themselves

One of the common things that people who work with XML do is to sort XML content based on values of attributes on XML elements, or according to the text contained in the elements. Sorting is useful for tables of data, but sometimes it is used for blocks of content like glossaries or directory listings. For example, with this XML:

```
<?xml version="1.0" encoding="UTF-8"?>
<glossary>
    <term>Affidavit</term>
    <definition>A legal document that provides proof (of residency, payment,
    status as an emancipated minor, etc.). Affidavits must be prepared by an
    attorney, appropriate agency or counselor, and must be attested to under
    supplied with a notarization stamp.</definition>
    <term>F-1 Visa</term>
    <definition>An F-1visa is a nonimmigrant visa issued by the USCIS (formerly
    INS) to the alien student who is pursuing studies in the US. The "F" visa
    is reserved for nonimmigrants wishing to pursue academic studies and/or
    language training programs.</definition>
    <term>INS documentation</term>
    <definition>Written materials provided by US Citizen and Immigration
    Services (formerly Immigration and Naturalization Services) to prove a
    student's status as an legal nonimmigrant.</definition>
    <term>Non-resident tuition rate</term>
    <definition>Students whose primary residence is not in the state will pay
    the tuition rate for non-residents. However, if a student resides within
    the state for the six months of the year immediately preceding the start
    of the session for which tuition is paid, the student qualifies for the
    resident tuition rate.</definition>
    <term>EDU-PAY</term>
    <definition>A payment plan for students who do not have the resources to
    pay the bill in full or who may not qualify for sufficient financial aid
    to cover the entire bill at the college.</definition>
</glossary>
```

you can use this XSL to write a top-level <glossary> element containing terms and definitions sorted in ascending alphabetical order:

```
<?xml version="1.0" encoding="UTF-8"?>
<xsl:stylesheet version="1.0" xmlns:xsl="http://www.w3.org/1999/XSL/Transform">
    <xsl:output method="xml" version="1.0" encoding="UTF-8"/>
    <xsl:template match="/">
        <xsl:element name="glossary">
            <xsl:for-each select="glossary/term">
              <xsl:sort order="ascending"/>
              <xsl:copy-of select="."/>
            <xsl:copy-of select="following-sibling::definition[1]"/>
            </xsl:for-each>
        </xsl:element>
    </xsl:template>
</xsl:stylesheet>
```

This is the resulting XML; the definition for EDU-PAY is now near the top of the list of terms instead of at the end.

```
<glossary>
    <term>Affidavit</term>
    <definition>A legal document that provides proof (of residency, payment,
    status as an emancipated minor, etc.). Affidavits must be prepared by an
    attorney, appropriate agency or counselor, and must be attested to under
    supplied with a notarization stamp.</definition>
    <term>EDU-PAY</term>
    <definition>A payment plan for students who do not have the resources to
    pay the bill in full or who may not qualify for sufficient financial aid
    to cover the entire bill at the college.</definition>
    <term>F-1 Visa</term>
    <definition>An F-1visa is a nonimmigrant visa issued by the USCIS (formerly
    INS) to the alien student who is pursuing studies in the US. The "F" visa
    is reserved for nonimmigrants wishing to pursue academic studies and/or
    language training programs.</definition>
    <term>INS documentation</term>
    <definition>Written materials provided by US Citizen and Immigration
    Services (formerly Immigration and Naturalization Services) to prove a
    student's status as an legal nonimmigrant.</definition>
    <term>Non-resident tuition rate</term>
    <definition>Students whose primary residence is not in the state will pay
    the tuition rate for non-residents. However, if a student resides within
    the state for the six months of the year immediately preceding the start
    of the session for which tuition is paid, the student qualifies for the
    resident tuition rate.</definition>
</glossary>
```

You can apply sorts that create descending order by using `xsl:sort order="descending"` on the elements you are looping over with the `<xsl:for-each>`. For more about loops and sorts, see *http://www.w3schools.com/xsl/el_sort.asp*.

To sort before importing XML into InDesign, apply the sorting transform, and then import the resulting XML output.

 For large documents, sorting when importing the XML (applying the XSL transform within the XML Import Options dialog) may make InDesign crash. Generally, best practice is to do sorting as a preprocessing step before importing XML.

XSL: Getting Rid of Elements You Don't Want

Excluding some of the elements can be accomplished with placeholders and the XML import option "Only import text elements that match existing structure" (see "Understanding InDesign's XML Import Options" (page 34)), but you might want to remove entire sets of elements, or only selected ones, on your way in or out of InDesign.

For example, let's suppose that you have product catalog XML that contains `<price>` elements that have both `<unit>` and `<bulk>` elements.[1] You produce two catalogs: one for wholesalers and one for consumers. You might use the same XML file for each catalog but suppress whichever price that doesn't apply in each catalog version.

Your XSL transform would look for the type of price you want in the catalog and copy only those products for import. This is the tiny example XML file, in which one element has a bulk price:

```
<?xml version="1.0" encoding="UTF-8"?>
<!-- <?xml-stylesheet type="text/xsl" href="bulkPrice.xsl"?> -->
<products>
    <product type="petToy">
        <name>Chewy Toy</name>
        <catno>D123</catno>
        <price currency="USD">
            <bulk qty="100">.39</bulk>
            <unit qty="1">.99</unit>
        </price>
        <unit pack="recyled" measure="imperial">4 oz.</unit>
        <description>Delicious enviro-friendly dog treat made with processed pig
          parts, shaped like a miniature pig.</description>
    </product>
    <product type="petToy">
        <name>Squeaky Toy</name>
        <catno>D456</catno>
        <price currency="USD">
            <unit qty="1">1.49</unit>
        </price>
        <unit pack="recyled" measure="imperial">5.1 oz.</unit>
        <description>Exciting enviro-friendly dog toy made with recycled,
          nontoxic, heavy-duty plastics. Squeak is air-produced, no hard parts
          inside. Safe for all mature dogs over 10 lbs. Not recommended for
          puppies and smaller dogs.</description>
    </product>
</products>
```

And here is a small XSL file that looks for a bulk price and copies only `<product>` elements that have one:

```
<?xml version="1.0" encoding="UTF-8"?>
<xsl:stylesheet version="1.0" xmlns:xsl="http://www.w3.org/1999/XSL/Transform">
    <xsl:output method="xml" version="1.0" standalone="yes"/>
    <xsl:template match="/">
        <xsl:apply-templates select="products"/>
    </xsl:template>
```

---

1. I'm momentarily tired of course catalog XML. Periodically, I have some fun imagining weird products like environmentally friendly pet toys. It's late. Forgive me.

```
<xsl:template match="products">
    <xsl:copy-of select="product[price/bulk !='']"/>
</xsl:template>
</xsl:stylesheet>
```

The previous example XSL produces this XML output:

```
<?xml version="1.0" encoding="UTF-16" standalone="yes"?>
<product type="petToy">
    <name>Chewy Toy</name>
    <catno>D123</catno>
    <price currency="USD">
        <bulk qty="100">.39</bulk>
        <unit qty="1">.99</unit>
    </price>
    <unit pack="recyled" measure="imperial">4 oz.</unit>
    <description>Delicious enviro-friendly dog treat made with processed pig
    parts, shaped like a miniature pig.</description>
</product>
```

In the previous example, the Squeaky Toy item was excluded because it doesn't have a bulk price. When the XML is imported into the wholesale catalog with the XSLT applied during import, the catalog content will be pertinent to the wholesale audience.

Alternately, you could process the original XML with XSL as a separate step before importing the XML into InDesign.

Creating Wrappers for Repeating Chunks

Sometimes you need to make a wrapper around part of the incoming XML to use the functions of InDesign placeholders or tables. With XSL, you can add an element to the original XML structure. Suppose you have a set of fairly complex elements that belong together, but they are just strung along one after another. In InDesign, you want to put each set into its own separate text flow. Here's an example of how you could make this happen with our previous glossary XML example:

```
<xsl:stylesheet version="1.0" xmlns:xsl="http://www.w3.org/1999/XSL/Transform">
    <xsl:output method="xml" version="1.0" encoding="UTF-8" indent="no"/>
    <xsl:template match="/">
        <xsl:element name="glossary">
            <xsl:for-each select="glossary/term">
                <!-- start the wrapper element inside the for-each loop so it
                    will make a wrapper for each term and definition pair -->
                <xsl:element name="glossTerm">
                    <xsl:copy-of select="."/>
                    <xsl:copy-of select="following-sibling::definition[1]"/>
                </xsl:element>
                <!-- end the wrapper element-->
```

```
        </xsl:for-each>
      </xsl:element>
    </xsl:template>
</xsl:stylesheet>
```

The resulting XML has a wrapper around each term and definition pair:

```
<?xml version="1.0" encoding="UTF-16"?>
<glossary>
    <glossTerm>
        <term>Affidavit</term>
        <definition>A legal document that provides proof (of residency, payment,
        status as an emancipated minor, etc.). Affidavits must be prepared by
        an attorney, appropriate agency or counselor, and must be attested to
        under supplied with a notarization stamp.</definition>
    </glossTerm>
    <glossTerm>
        <term>F-1 Visa</term>
        <definition>An F-1visa is a nonimmigrant visa issued by the USCIS
        (formerly INS) to the alien student who is pursuing studies in the US.
        The "F" visa is reserved for nonimmigrants wishing to pursue academic
        studies and/or language training programs.</definition>
    </glossTerm>
    <glossTerm>
        <term>INS documentation</term>
        <definition>Written materials provided by US Citizen and Immigration
        Services (formerly Immigration and Naturalization Services) to prove a
        student's status as an legal nonimmigrant.</definition>
    </glossTerm>
    <glossTerm>
        <term>Non-resident tuition rate</term>
        <definition>Students whose primary residence is not in the state will
        pay the tuition rate for non-residents. However, if a student resides
        within the state for the six months of the year immediately preceding
        the start of the session for which tuition is paid, the student
        qualifies for the resident tuition rate.</definition>
    </glossTerm>
    <glossTerm>
        <term>EDU-PAY</term>
        <definition>A payment plan for students who do not have the
        resources to pay the bill in full or who may not qualify for sufficient
        financial aid to cover the entire bill at the college.</definition>
    </glossTerm>
</glossary>
```

If you have a text frame for each glossTerm, you can drag each of the terms into its text frame. Or you can create a glossary as a text flow tagged as <glossary> that you set up previously for repeating block placeholder elements structured like this: an element called <glossTerm>, containing the <term> element, followed by a manual line break, then a tab and a <definition> element, followed by a paragraph break. See Figure 10-3.

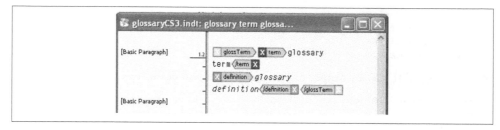

Figure 10-3. Placeholders (shown in Story Editor view) including the wrapper element that will be created with the XSLT

The `<term>` and `<definition>` elements are mapped to character styles to make them bold and italic, respectively. The `<glossTerm>` element is mapped to a Basic Paragraph style.

The XML Import Options dialog should look like Figure 10-4, pointing to the XSLT. The results will look like Figure 10-5 in InDesign.

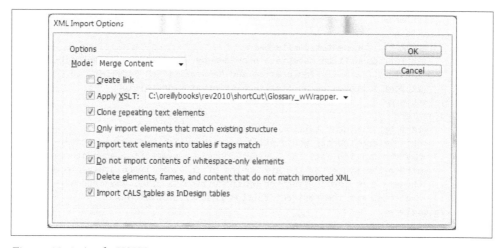

Figure 10-4. Apply XSLT to create wrappers on import

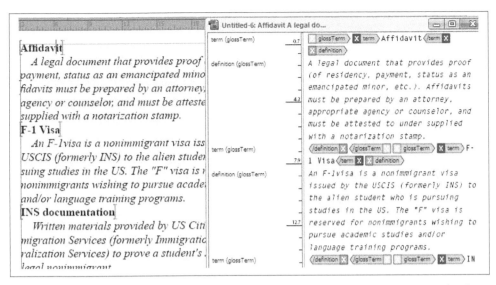

Figure 10-5. Example of creating wrapper elements with XSLT on import with place-holders for repeating blocks of content

By extrapolation, any time you need to make a repeating block, the same XSLT technique can be used to develop richer XML with the required wrapper elements.

Making a Table from Element Structures

Let's use the same kind of concept to make an InDesign table from our incoming XML. In this example, suppose that we do not want to have `<Table>` and `<Cell>` elements in our source XML because it violates our DTD. We can add the table markup solely within InDesign and keep our XML source pure. We will use XSLT upon import into InDesign.

We'll go back to the InDesign placeholder concept first and make a table that looks like what we want to generate (this is always the best practice if you need to make tables from XML in InDesign). Our simple table looks like Figure 10-6: the table is tagged as `<glossary>` and consists of a header row containing two cells tagged as `<colHead>` elements and another row containing one cell tagged as `<term>` and one tagged as `<definition>`.

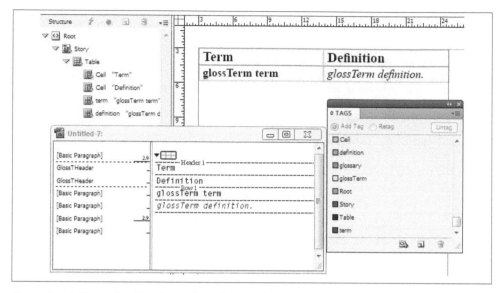

Figure 10-6. Tagged table placeholder for the glossary

InDesign doesn't use "rows" in its internal table model. So the table setup does not need anything tagged as `<glossTerm>` (which would map to a table row logically) as a container for the term and definition pair.

Now we can use this XSLT upon import by selecting it in the Import XML dialog using the Apply XSLT option:

```
<?xml version="1.0" encoding="UTF-8"?>
<xsl:stylesheet version="1.0" xmlns:xsl="http://www.w3.org/1999/XSL/Transform">
    <xsl:template match="/">
        <xsl:element name="glossary">
            <xsl:for-each select="glossary/term">
                <!-- start the wrapper element inside the for-each loop so it
                    will make a wrapper for each term and definition pair -->
                <xsl:element name="glossTerm">
                    <xsl:copy-of select="."/>
                    <xsl:copy-of select="following-sibling::definition[1]"/>
                </xsl:element>
                <!-- end the wrapper element-->
            </xsl:for-each>
        </xsl:element>
    </xsl:template>
</xsl:stylesheet>
```

By applying the XSLT on the glossary XML, we get the table shown in Figure 10-7 in InDesign.

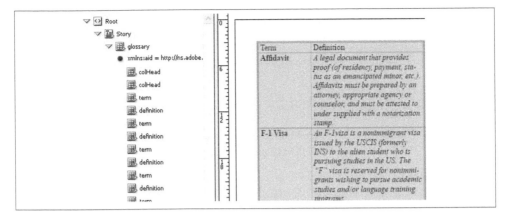

Figure 10-7. Table with multiple rows created by importing XML into InDesign with XSLT

If you set up the table with heading rows, they will repeat when the table flows from one text frame to another. If you use the alternate row coloring, you can achieve a look like Figure 10-8.

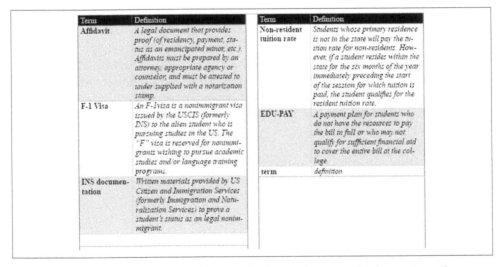

Figure 10-8. Imported table flowed into multiple text frames with alternating color

See the InDesign Help section on tables for more information on creating the look you want in your table layout.

If you want to use tables to make run-in heads (similar to how many people do it in Microsoft Word), turn off the rules and shading in the table styles in InDesign. To make true run-in heads in InDesign, follow the directions in the InDesign Help for nested styles.

Upcasting Versus Downcasting

In XSLT, changing simple XML or HTML to a more complex XML form is *upcasting* and changing XML to a simpler DTD is *downcasting*.

It may be that you need to convert HTML content into some form of XML. The simplest way to do this is to save your HTML as XHTML, a form of HTML that conforms to XML rules. Once it has been cleaned up as XHTML, you need to change the file extension to *.xml* before you import it into InDesign.

 You can use an open source utility application called HTML Tidy (*http://tidy.sourceforge.net/#binaries*) to make valid XHTML from your web page content. It is also bundled with Adobe Dreamweaver and some other applications that you may be using. Check for the ability to save web content as XHTML or HTML 4.0, also know as "strict" HTML.

It is possible to import the XHTML file without any transformation, but we want to modify the incoming XML somewhat to make it more compatible with our InDesign layout. We will model the XHTML elements that correspond to the InDesign tagging concepts. We don't necessarily need the <head> element, because it is used only for the HTML title bar and metadata, not for anything that we will print. So we can make a structure like Figure 10-9 in InDesign.

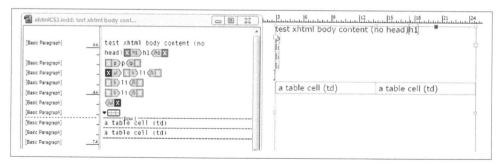

Figure 10-9. Placeholder for XHTML import

Remember that you can use XSLT to change the order of elements (such as sorting alphabetically), but this step is best done as a preprocessing step before importing XML, rather than using the Apply XSLT option.

 To make the import process format imported XML text automatically, create paragraph styles that match the names of the XHTML elements (h1, p, li, etc.) and use Map Tags to Styles with the Map By Name box checked to apply the paragraph styles to the placeholder elements before you import the XML.

To make the XHTML `<table>` element, which is always a lowercase word, match to InDesign's internal tag `<Table>`), which is always uppercase, we will use the Tagging Presets dialog on the Tags panel (see Figure 10-10). We also want the `<td>` element to map to the InDesign `<Cell>`.

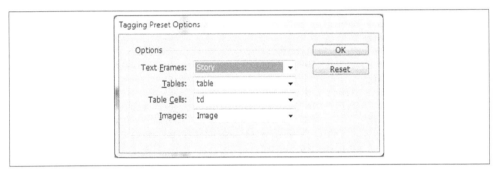

Figure 10-10. The Tagging Preset Options of the Tags panel, setting Tables and Table Cells to <table> and <td> elements

In my tests, I used a simple XHTML file that looked like this:

```
<?xml version="1.0" encoding="UTF-8"?>
<!-- <?xml-stylesheet type="text/xsl" href="xmlizeXHTML.xslt"?> -->
<html>
    <head>
        <title>XHTML example</title>
    </head>
    <body>
        <h1>An example of XHTML</h1>
        <p>Some general rules for XHTML are</p>
        <ul>
            <li>Every start tag must have a matching end tag</li>
            <li>All tag pairs must end without crossing over other end tags
                (to create properly nested structures)</li>
```

```
                <li>Tag names cannot start with a number, and they cannot include
                    any spaces, or "illegal" characters, such as  ? and /, which
                    can be confused with parts of the markup and processing
                    instructions.</li>
            </ul>
            <table border="1">
                <tbody>
                    <tr><th>a table header (th)</th></tr>
                    <tr><td>a table cell (td)</td></tr>
                </tbody>
            </table>
        </body>
    </html>
```

The XSLT that we will use to simplify the XHTML looks like this (although this example
is not developed to handle all possible XHTML elements):

```
<?xml version="1.0" encoding="UTF-8"?>
<xsl:stylesheet version="1.0" xmlns:xsl="http://www.w3.org/1999/XSL/Transform">
    <xsl:output method="xml" version="1.0" encoding="UTF-8" indent="yes"/>
    <xsl:template match="/">
        <xsl:apply-templates select="html/body"></xsl:apply-templates>
    </xsl:template>
    <xsl:template match="html/body">
    <xsl:element name="body"><xsl:apply-templates/></xsl:element>
    </xsl:template>
    <!-- copy some elements directly -->
    <xsl:template match="h1|h2|h3|h4|h5|h6|p|ul|ol"><xsl:copy-of select="."/>
    </xsl:template>
    <!-- simplify the table structure to what InDesign uses,
        no tbody or tr elements needed -->
    <xsl:template match="table">
        <xsl:element name="Table"><xsl:apply-templates/></xsl:element>
    </xsl:template>
    <xsl:template match="tbody"><xsl:apply-templates select="tr"/>
    </xsl:template>
    <xsl:template match="tr"><xsl:apply-templates select="th|td"/>
    </xsl:template>
    <xsl:template match="th"><xsl:element name="Cell"><xsl:apply-templates/>
    </xsl:element>
    </xsl:template>
    <xsl:template match="td"><xsl:copy-of select="."/></xsl:template>
    <xsl:template match="img">
        <xsl:element name="Image"><xsl:attribute name="href">
         <xsl:value-of select="@href"/></xsl:attribute></xsl:element>
    </xsl:template>
    <!-- exclude the head tag content -->
    <xsl:template match="html/head"/>
</xsl:stylesheet>
```

We can import the XML and apply the XSLT to it as it comes in. Doing so will strip off the unnecessary `<head>` element and simplify the `<table>` by removing the `<tbody>` and `<tr>` tags. Select the `<body>` placeholder element in the structure view and use File→Import XML, then select the XHTML file that you saved with a .xml extension.

 The import operation sometimes crashed when I selected an `<html>` element in the placeholder as the element to import into. Importing worked when I selected the `<body>` tag as the location to import the XML, possibly because we are creating an XML file that uses the `<body>` element as its root. At any rate, be forewarned that importing and applying XSLT can be fraught with peril—save a copy of the file with placeholders or make it an InDesign template before you start applying XSLT while importing XML.

The settings for the XML Import Options dialog will be: Apply XSLT, "Clone repeating text elements" (for the ul/li structure), "Only import elements that match existing structure" *(it is important to check this)*, and "Do not import contents of whitespace-only elements"; see Figure 10-11.

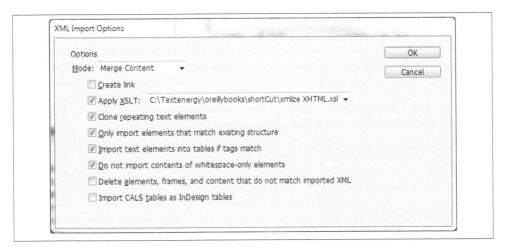

Figure 10-11. Settings for the XML Import Options dialog for the XHTML-as-XML import

The results, after some tinkering with the Paragraph styles, are shown in Figure 10-12.

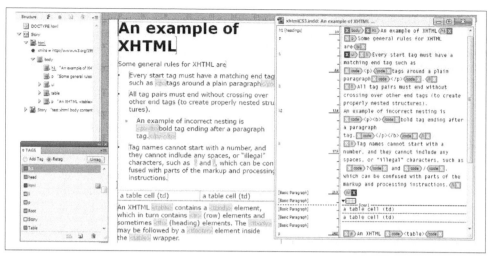

Figure 10-12. XHTML imported into InDesign and formatted with matching paragraph and character styles

Upcasting from HTML to XML for InDesign Import

You can extend this concept to all the tags in the official XHTML DTD, if you wish. Generally, you would want to use XSLT for the following tasks:

- To remove unnecessary structure that InDesign doesn't use (such as the <head>, <tbody>, and <tr> elements)

- To wrap elements that you want to have treated as repeating blocks (such as <ul> or <ol> elements that contain <li> elements)

- To change names of elements to match InDesign's built-in names (such as Table and Cell)

Downcasting to HTML

In some cases (although who would ever want to do this?), you might want to save some XML in InDesign as web page content that matches a particular CSS. You can do this by saving the content with an XSLT written to downcast the XML structure to standard HTML tags. (See also the section "Exporting XHTML When XML is in Your InDesign File" (page 29).) Let's try the XSLT export to HTML with the course descriptions that we have worked with earlier.

First, we must decide what the output for the HTML will be. We'll assume that we have a CSS already set up for displaying the course descriptions online. To make it simple to understand, the CSS classes have names that correlate to the XML elements.

I recommend that you always use class names that will help you remember the XML element origin of the HTML output. If you solely use the <h1>, <h2>, and <p> tags, you will later be unable to differentiate the HTML produced from <CourseDescriptions> from any other HTML except by reading the text for meaning. These types of semantic class names also may have benefit to help search engines as HTML "microformats" become more widely used.

We are going to create a new XHTML output from the course content using a series of steps. We can use the same tags that we created for the XHTML example for this example. We already have a simple tagged file with <h1>, <p>, <ul>, <li>, <p>, and <code> elements in a <body> element, which we can export to get an idea of the result file that we want. Select the XML in the Structure pane, then right-click to get the Structure menu and select Export XML. In the export dialog, use the settings in Figure 10-13.

Figure 10-13. The Export XML dialog with options set to make quasi-XHTML output

The box for "Remap Break, Whitespace, and Special Characters" must be checked to clean up typographic characters that will not display in a browser properly (line returns, pretty quotes, em dashes, ampersands, etc.).

After you export, change the file extension of the exported file from *.xml* to *.html* and see how it looks in your browser; see Figure 10-14. (For our example, which did not have a <head> element, you must edit the output file if you want to make it conform to the HTML strict DTD. See *http:/w3cschools.org* for good tutorials on XHTML.)

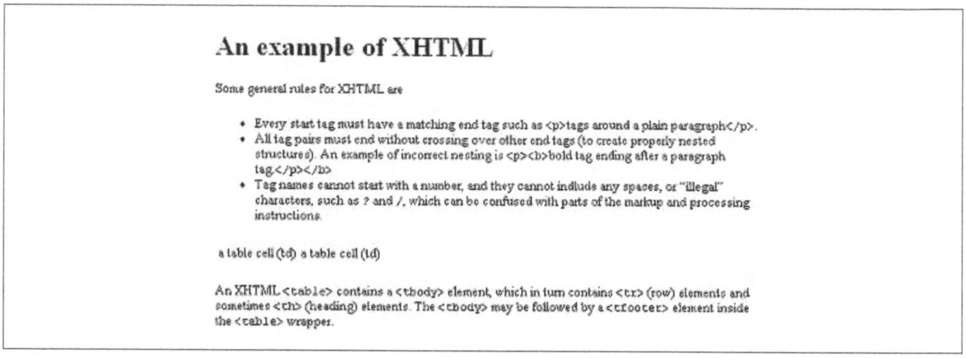

An example of XHTML

Some general rules for XHTML are

- Every start tag must have a matching end tag such as <p>tags around a plain paragraph</p>.
- All tag pairs must end without crossing over other end tags (to create properly nested structures). An example of incorrect nesting is <p><b>bold tag ending after a paragraph tag.</p></b>
- Tag names cannot start with a number, and they cannot include any spaces, or "illegal" characters, such as ? and /, which can be confused with parts of the markup and processing instructions.

a table cell (td) a table cell (td)

An XHTML <table> contains a <tbody> element, which in turn contains <tr> (row) elements and sometimes <th> (heading) elements. The <tbody> may be followed by a <tfooter> element inside the <table> wrapper.

Figure 10-14. The XHTML export (cleaned to conform to the HTML strict DTD)

Compare the course content to the HTML tags to see how you might want to tag the final output. For example, you might want to output the element <CourseDescrip tions_Major> as an <h1 class="major">, and the <CourseDescription_Name> as an <h2 class="coursename">, the <CourseDescription_Text> as <p class="coursede scription">, and the prerequisite <CourseDescription_Note> as <p class="course note">. The semantically meaningful CSS class names will help make apparent the subject of the content and its origin.

This is the sample XML:

```
<CourseDescriptions>
    <CourseDescription_Major>Accounting</CourseDescription_Major>
    <CourseDescription>
        <CourseDescription_Name>ACC 101&#9;Accounting Principles I&#9;4 Credits
        </CourseDescription_Name>
        <CourseDescription_Text>Basic principles of financial accounting for
            the business enterprise with emphasis on the valuation of business
            assets, measurement of net income, and double-entry techniques for
            recording transactions.  Introduction to the cycle of accounting
            work, preparation of financial statements, and adjusting and closing
            procedures.  Four class hours.</CourseDescription_Text>
        <CourseDescription_Footnote type="prereq">
            Prerequisite: MTH 098 or MTH 130 or equivalent.
        </CourseDescription_Footnote>
    </CourseDescription>
    ...
    <CourseDescription_Major>Art</CourseDescription_Major>
    <CourseDescription>
        <CourseDescription_Name>ART 101    Art Essentials    3 Credits
```

```
        </CourseDescription_Name>
    <CourseDescription_Text>This course is designed to improve the student's
        visual perception and expand critical awareness through a variety of
        hands-on studio projects. The student will become familiar with the
        methods, materials, media, vocabulary, and techniques of making art.
        This course is suggested for students who are interested in
        developing their creative skills but are not art majors.
        Two class hours, two studio hours. (SUNY-A)
    </CourseDescription_Text>
  </CourseDescription>
</CourseDescriptions>
```

The XSL transform could accomplish these XML to HTML changes: generate a valid
`<html>` with `<head>`, `<title>` `<link>` (for the CSS file) and `<body>`, and then make the
individual heading levels with the CSS classes and even some IDs. Example 10-1 is a
simple XSLT example without any loops.

Example 10-1. courseDescriptions2HTML.xsl

```
<?xml version="1.0" encoding="UTF-8"?>
<xsl:stylesheet version="1.0" xmlns:xsl="http://www.w3.org/1999/XSL/Transform">
    <xsl:output method="html" encoding="utf-8"/>
    <xsl:template match="/">
        <html>
            <head>
                <title>Course descriptions web version</title>
                <link rel="stylesheet" href="courses.css"    type="text/css"></link>
            </head>
            <body>
                <xsl:apply-templates/>
            </body>
        </html>
    </xsl:template>
    <xsl:template match="CourseDescriptions">
        <h1>Course Descriptions</h1>
        <xsl:apply-templates/>
    </xsl:template>
    <xsl:template match="CourseDescription">
        <div>
            <xsl:attribute name="id">
              <xsl:value-of select="substring(CourseDescription_Name,1,7)"/>
              <xsl:apply-templates/></xsl:attribute>
            <xsl:apply-templates/>
        </div>
    </xsl:template>
    <xsl:template match="CourseDescription_Major">
        <hr/>
        <div class="major">
            <xsl:attribute name="id"><xsl:value-of select="."/></xsl:attribute>
            <h2 class="major">
                <xsl:value-of select="."/>
            </h2>
```

```
        </div>
    </xsl:template>
    <xsl:template match="CourseDescription_Name">
        <h3 class="coursename">
            <xsl:value-of select="."/>
        </h3>
    </xsl:template>
    <xsl:template match="CourseDescription_Text">
        <p class="coursedescription">
            <xsl:value-of select="."/>
        </p>
    </xsl:template>
    <xsl:template match="CourseDescription_Footnote">
        <p class="coursenote">
            <xsl:text>Notes: </xsl:text><br/>
            <xsl:value-of select="."/>
        </p>
    </xsl:template>
</xsl:stylesheet>
```

The CSS has only a few classes in it:

```
body
{background-color: #ffffff;}
h1, h2, h3 {font-family: Verdana, Arial, sans-serif;;margin-bottom:6px}
.major {color:green; font-size: 19px;margin-bottom:0px}
.coursename {color:navy; font-size: 13px;margin-bottom:0px}
p {font-family: Arial, Verdana, sans-serif; font-style:normal; font-size: 13px}
.coursedescription {font-style:normal;color:#000000;margin:0px 0px 0px 0px}
.coursenote {font-style:italic;color:#333333;margin: 0px 10px 20px 20px}
```

The HTML output looks like Figure 10-15 (viewed in the browser to see the CSS applied).

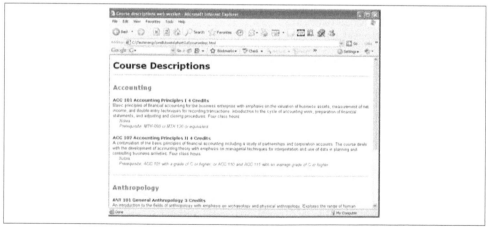

Figure 10-15. XHTML created from XML exported using Apply XSLT to add CSS styles

Notice that the course numbers have been used to generate unique IDs for the `<div>`s containing course descriptions:

```html
<html>
<head>
    <META http-equiv="Content-Type" content="text/html; charset=utf-8" />
    <title>Course descriptions web version</title>
    <link rel="stylesheet" href="courses.css" type="text/css" />
</head>
<body>
    <h1>Course Descriptions</h1>
    <hr>
    <div class="major" id="Accounting">
    <h2 class="major">Accounting</h2>
    </div>
    <div id="ACC 101">
    <h3 class="coursename">ACC 101&#9;Accounting Principles I&#9;4 Credits</h3>
    <p class="coursedescription">Basic principles of financial accounting for
        the business enterprise with emphasis on the valuation of business
        assets, measurement of net income, and double-entry techniques for
        recording transactions. Introduction to the cycle of accounting work,
        preparation of financial statements, and adjusting and closing
        procedures. Four class hours.</p>
    <p class="coursenote">Notes: <br>Prerequisite: MTH 098 or MTH 130
    or equivalent.</p>
    </div>
    ...more
    <hr>
    <div class="major" id="Art">
    <h2 class="major">Art</h2>
    </div>
    <div id="ART 101">
    <h3 class="coursename">ART 101    Art Essentials    3 Credits</h3>
    <p class="coursedescription">This course is designed to improve the
        student's visual perception and expand critical awareness through a
        variety of hands-on studio projects. The student will become familiar
        with the methods, materials, media, vocabulary, and techniques of making
        art. This course is suggested for students who are interested in
        developing their creative skills but are not art majors.  Two class
        hours, two studio hours. (SUNY-A)</p>
    </div>
</body>
</html>
```

To get HTML, I used the XSLT on export, but it took a few trials to get it to work. It generated some error messages that require some fairly deep understanding of XSLT to fix. It sometimes crashed if I tried to do anything too fancy with sorting or rearranging the XML. And, I could only name the exported file with the *.xml* file extension.

However, Adobe has included some nice features in the XHTML export. Check the online documentation, including videos, that Adobe provides about XHTML export from InDesign (*http://tv.adobe.com*). One of the options is to add empty CSS classes to content as you export it. Then, you can add the kind of semantic names that I am suggesting if it is worthwhile to help you remember the source of the content. Or you can use a CSS that you already have for your website and forget the semantics. So if XSLT is too daunting, why bother? Just create XHTML directly. Thanks, Adobe. (I think. You won't get to do all the cool things that XSLT can offer, but that may be overkill for a lot of folks. Just because I love XML and XSLT doesn't mean that everyone else has to suffer for it.)

Generate a Link with XSLT (Not Automated)

Have you noticed that I haven't mentioned anything about links in my discussion of generating XHTML with XSLT? Adobe has enabled an auto-generation of hyperlinks in InDesign (if you use the Cross Media Export→Export to XHTML, I believe the <a> tag will be created from a hyperlink you have created with a URL). But, if you are writing your own XSLT, there is no built-in method to get the <a> tag in the Export XML output. The most straightforward way to handle it is to create a standard web <a> tag in your content, give it an href attribute, and export it.

If your current InDesign XML tag set doesn't include the <a> tag, you can add it to the list of tags. In the Tags window, select New tag, then overtype the highlighted tag name in the window with "a". Switch to the Text Selection tool, select the text you want to use for your link, and tag it by clicking the new <a> tag name in the Tags list.

You must add the required href attribute to the <a>-tagged text. With the tagged text selected in the Structure pane, click the round black button in the top of the Structure window. When the Add Attribute window opens, type "href " (without quotes) in the name text box and the destination URL in the value text box.

To get this element in your export when you are using Apply XSLT, include a small template that copies the <a> tag, including its attribute:

```
<xsl:template match="a"><xsl:copy-of select="."/></xsl:template>
```

With XSLT, you can also rewrite an existing element such as <link> to an <a> element with an empty @href attribute. Then you can edit the @href in an HTML editor to insert the correct link path and file name. More advanced XSLT can use automation to pass in a relative path to a known website location and prepend it into the @href value. For example, you can have a parameter in your XSLT, $mysite, defined as *http:// www.mysite.com/*, then insert that as the starting part of every @href. Then all you would have to do is add the correct filename for the *.html* page or other resources that your @href points to.

Adding Useful Attributes to XML

Attributes are little descriptive bits of information used by programs and people to find and manipulate items in XML files. You can add attributes to indicate:

- The status of development (draft, revision, final, approved)
- The audience or type of user who would want a piece of content (novice, expert, user, service operator, etc.)
- The currency of monetary values
- Whatever will help you work with your XML content

Generally, it is easier to add attributes with XSLT than within InDesign if you want to use them all over your XML, but Adobe gives you a tool to add an attribute manually, so we'll start with that.

Select an XML element in the Structure pane, then click the big black dot in the top icon bar of the Structure pane (or right-click and select New Attribute from the Structure menu). In the New Attribute dialog, enter the name of the attribute and the value (Figure 10-16).

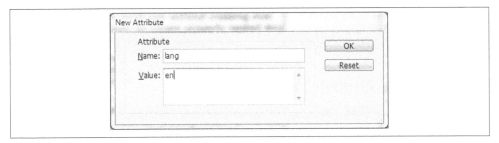

Figure 10-16. The New Attribute dialog used to add the lang attribute

Adobe should have included the ability to add standard attributes for lang, whitespace handling, and other attributes that people who work with XML commonly use. Because these are not available with any kind of menu or picker in InDesign, you have to add them manually or with XSLT.

A General Formula for Adding Attributes

Here is a general formula for XSL templates to add an attribute to your XML:

```
<xsl:attribute name="attname">attvalue</xsl:attribute>
```

where attname is the name of the attribute and attvalue is the value you want to assign to that attribute. In my course descriptions XSL example, I used a generated value in several places. This template takes a part of the text string (characters 1–7) that is contained in a <CourseDescription_Name> and uses that as the value of the id attribute that is being added to a div, such as <div id="ACC 101">; see Example 10-2.

Example 10-2. An XSL template to capture a substring (selected part of element text)

```
<xsl:template match="CourseDescription">
    <div>
        <xsl:attribute name="id"><xsl:value-of select="substring(
            CourseDescription_Name,1,7)"/><xsl:apply-templates/>
        </xsl:attribute>
        <xsl:apply-templates/>
    </div>
</xsl:template>
```

 The substring operation seemed prone to crashes when I used it with Apply XSLT when importing XML. It might be better to apply the XSLT to the XML as a preprocessing step when you want to do string operations with your transforms.

Generating an id Attribute for a div

In the next template, the value of the <CourseDescription_Major> element is being used to generate the div's id value, such as <div id="Accounting">. The dot in the xls:value-of select="." will be replaced with the word Accounting (the dot notation means "self," or the current element's content). See Figure 10-17.

```
<xsl:template match="CourseDescription_Major">
    <hr/>
    <div class="major">
        <xsl:attribute name="id"><xsl:value-of select="."/></xsl:attribute>
        <h2 class="major">
            <xsl:value-of select="."/>
        </h2>
    </div>
</xsl:template>
```

Figure 10-17. An XSL template to generate a div id from element text

Use of the lang Attribute for Translations

For the sake of multilingual content, you might want to add an attribute of `lang` to the root element of your XML file. The general syntax for the attribute is `<elementname lang="en">` (or `lang="es"` for Spanish, `lang="de"` for German, `lang="it"` for Italian, etc.). It can be important to know whether the content is American English or British English (for instance, to know what the measurement units should be), so the approved country codes can be appended to the lang code, as `en-us` or `en-gb`.

If you are writing content that mixes in some words, phrases, or quotations in other languages, you might think about marking these up as inline elements (keyword, glossterm, or some other element), and using a `lang` attribute to indicate that the content is in a different language. For example, Latin names in scientific or medical texts, Spanish song titles in a music catalog, or French words in a cookbook could all be treated in this manner.

> If an entire block element like a `<p>`, `<div>`, or `<table>` should be marked as a different language, put the `lang` attribute on the element rather than adding an inline element with a `lang` attribute.

Conversely, if there is text that you do not want to have translated, such as company names, slogans, trade, and brand names, you could use `lang="en"` and add another attribute such as `translate="no"` on the same word or phrase, such as `<keyword lang="en" translate="no">Textenergy LLC</keyword>`.

> If you think ahead about attribute issues at the time you create your XML, you can save a lot of money on translation costs.

Creating an Image href Attribute

If you want to import graphics, the XML element that will contain your image needs an attribute named `href` and the path and filename of the graphics file.

The XSL transform is pretty simple—the name of your element (`<Image>`, `<myBanner>`, `<logo>`, or whatever)—you add code in the template for that element to append the `href` attribute to the element:

```
<xsl:attribute name="href">file://path/filename.ext
</xsl:attribute>
```

Here, `href` is the *required* name of the attribute, and you replace `file://path/file name.ext` with the path (which can be many folders long) and the filename of your graphics file. You can even leave the basic XSL template with this boilerplate `file:// path/filename.ext` in it; it will create a valid placeholder for the image and then you can fill in the correct path and filename later if you don't know it at the time you create the XML for import. (This is often the case when someone says that you will have artwork for certain places in your document but hasn't provided the actual images yet. Once you know which image goes where, and what the path and filename is, adding images into your XML is a simple as writing the correct `href` value.)

Paths to images

If the folder where your images are located is known, you can write the path as part of the XSLT template. Just replace the path boilerplate with the real path, so it reads as:

```
<xsl:attribute name="href">file:///C:/test/images/filename.ext
</xsl:attribute>
```

or whatever drive and folders you need to point to. Just realize that you are hardcoding it in, so if you move the graphics to a different location, the links will break, and the image won't show up in the InDesign layout. Use three slashes for absolute filepaths (`file:///C:/`).

If you plan to export your InDesign file later, use the image files' relative path, such as:

```
<xsl:attribute name="href">file://images/filename.ext
</xsl:attribute>.
```

(In this example, the *images* folder is below your InDesign document folder, but it should be whatever your actual relative path is to replace `//images`.)

A Word about Using Find/Change for XML Markup in InDesign

You can use Edit→Find/Change as a means of locating specific types of styling in your document that you would like to mark up as XML elements. The process is described in the Adobe InDesign Technical Reference documentation, available on the Adobe website. The Find/Change dialog has an expression language that lets you write a pattern to search for and a pattern to replace the found text. Using the Find/Change dialog, you can select an XML element to apply from the Tags list (the tags must already be available in your InDesign document, either from using Load Tags or Load DTD).

This method can be very helpful for applying or fixing up XML markup, such as when you decide to change the name of an XML element after it has been applied. A common example is to search for a bold override or a character style that applies bold to the underlying text and tag it as the element <b>. (I would not recommend using Find/Change if you are working with a *linked* XML file that you have imported into InDesign.)

 Always save a copy of your InDesign file before using Find/Change to alter or add XML markup.

There is no mechanism for adding an attribute to an element using Find/Change, and you can't search for specific XML tags and change their names with the Find/Change dialog.

Content Model Depth Issues and Their Impact on Round-Tripping XML

InDesign is a shallow content model when it comes to text and images on a page. There are *no* built-in XML tags for titles, lists, extracts, figure captions, and other element. So any XML structure that you create for text has to be modeled in an InDesign template or imported as a DTD to create tag names in the Tags panel.

Even more limiting is that there is no concept of text divisions such as chapter, sections, sidebars, notes, and so on. From an InDesign point of view, everything is a paragraph or a run of styled text within a paragraph; it wouldn't make sense to "nest" a paragraph inside a paragraph. All of the deep structure of XML is superfluous to InDesign's tasks of making nice-looking text on a page.

Despite these limitations, many people are trying to read and write complex XML within InDesign.

The Challenge of Mapping Deep DTDs to Shallow InDesign Structures

It is possible to transform the deep content structures of DocBook or DITA XML to paragraph and character styles. See "Upcasting Versus Downcasting" (page 90) and "Downcasting to HTML" (page 94) for explanations of the downcasting process used to flatten XML structure. The challenge here is the proliferation of styles required for enabling the upcasting that will be performed later. For example: in the XML, there may be an element called `title` at many different levels in the structure. In InDesign, you want the title to be styled according to its relative position in the hierarchy, its context. If it is the title of a `<chapter>`, then you want it to become a paragraph styled as "CH-T". If it is the title of a first-level `<sect1>` element, you want it to become a paragraph styled as "Sect1-T". If it is the title of a `<glossary>`, then you want it to become a paragraph styled as "GLS-T", and so on. So you have a one-to-many relationship from the `<title>` element to the InDesign content, for which you can use XSLT to apply the required `aid:` namespace to generate the styles on the XML, according to the context of the `<title>` in the XML structure. (See "The Special Case of InDesign Tables (Namespaced XML)" (page 49) for a description of the `aid:` namespace.)

> To use the `aid:` namespace when validating in your XML in InDesign, you must add it to the DTD. Generally this means that the namespaced attribute must be added to all the elements that you need to map to styles in InDesign. See the section "4.4. Namespaces and DTDs" in *XML in a Nutshell*, 2nd ed. (O'Reilly, 2002) for a discussion.
>
> You can use the InDesign DTD itself for developing a flattened form of XML instead of adding support for the `aid:` namespace to an existing DTD. The InDesign DTDs are in the InDesign Developer's SDK, which is available from Adobe.

For XSLT developers: An XSLT for inserting the styles can be written with a set of templates for `<chapter>`, `<sect1>`, and `<glossary>` that adds the `aid:pstyle` with the desired paragraph style to the title. A more robust approach is to write a template for the `<title>` element that is called within the templates for `<chapter>`, `<sect1>`, and `<glossary>` using `xsl:apply-templates`, that passes the context of the `<title>` to an `xsl:choose` statement. The result should be `<title aid:pstyle="CH-T">`, `<title aid:pstyle="Sect1-T">`, `<title aid:pstyle="GLS-T">`, and so on.

The Challenge of Mapping Shallow Structures to Deep DTD Structures

When you have the same element with different `aid:pstyle` values, you can use the logic of the `aid:pstyle` during upcasting to restore a deeper structure from a flat InDesign structure. It is not foolproof and takes some care in naming the styles. You would export the InDesign XML that has the `aid:` namespace attributes and transform it with XSLT with logic that creates the "container" elements required. For example, based on the exported InDesign XML having a `<title aid:pstyle="CH-T">`, you first generate the wrapper element `<chapter>` and then within it generate the `<title>` element. Similarly, you generate the `<sect1>` containing a `<title>` from the `<title aid:pstyle="Sect1-T">`.

The inherent problem in this approach is the content editing that may go on after the XML is inside InDesign. If a new set of elements is created after the initial XML import, those new elements won't automatically take on the styles in InDesign, because it is during the import process that InDesign uses the `aid:` namespace. So the new content needs to have both XML structure markup and InDesign styles applied when it is created in InDesign. Then the correct `aid:` attribute values must be added to the new XML elements so that when the XML is exported, those elements will have the "hook" to restore the deeper XML content structure.

It will be extremely important that the people working on the InDesign files containing the XML understand these issues and how to maintain the `aid:` attribute values for each element according to where it is used.

An alternate approach is to have elaborate InDesign scripts that run on the XML and check the style name and apply the necessary `aid:` namespace attribute values for any XML elements that don't have them before the XML is exported from InDesign. These scripts can use a mapping logic to check where the new element has been inserted and what style has been applied to it and then create the `aid:` attribute as needed. This level of programming will require an experienced InDesign developer with knowledge of both the InDesign SDK and XML.

Use of Semantic ids and Style Names (Expert-Level Development)

An improvement over the use of the `aid:` namespace alone is to use both an `id` value and a styling attribute value in the XML to help with a parallel upcasting and downcasting scenario (round-tripping). For example, in DITA XML, you can have an id on most elements, and you can have an `outputclass` attribute. You can develop a systematic use of the combination of the `id` and the `outputclass` naming conventions to help keep track of the XML content going in and out of InDesign.

An example is having a title element whose `id` includes some type of "context" information and the desired InDesign styling such as `<title id="ch01" outputclass="CH-T">`, `<title id="ch01-sect1-01" outputclass="Sect1-T">`, and `<title id="ch01-glossary-01" outputclass="GLS-T">`. During downcasting, the ids are copied onto the XML elements that will be placed in InDesign, and the outputclass attribute values are used to generate the `aid:` namespace attribute values. This approach keeps more of the context for the future downcasting *as long as the id values are never changed*. During downcasting, the original XML file can be used as an input, compared to the exported XML. If a matching `id` value is found, then the exported XML is processed to put it into the same XML structure as the original XML. A set of templates will be required in the XSLT to handle unmatched content, but if the `id` values have been maintained during import and export, it will be possible to reconstruct the majority of the deeper XML structure.

The same concept can be used with DocBook XML files. Note how the `id` and `aid:` values are carried over from DocBook to InDesign in the examples in Figure 11-1.

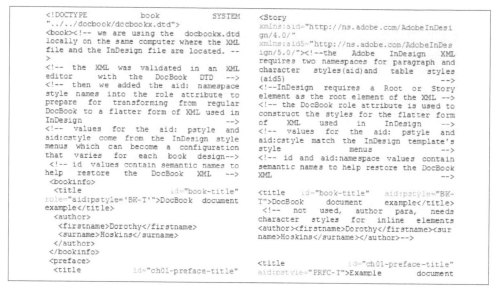

Figure 11-1. Comparison of DocBook and InDesign XML with aid: and aid5: namespaces

In Figure 11-1, I made use of DocBook's `role` attribute to insert the `aid:` namespace values. If the `role` attribute is needed for other functions in the DocBook content, then it may be best to add support for the `aid:` namespace attributes directly to the DocBook DTD.

The `aid:` namespace attribute values must match the InDesign style names and the InDesign template must be set up for the XML tags for the styling to be applied when the XML is placed in the layout.

A fully developed DocBook XML file, InDesign template, and XSLT would use an `id` on every paragraph (and conceivably on every inline element), whose value could be made unique by using the `generate-id()` function. In the example in Figure 11-2, more semantic names assist the reader of this book to follow the relationship between the DocBook and InDesign XML. The InDesign template in Figure 11-2 has a unique paragraph style for each of the different title types.

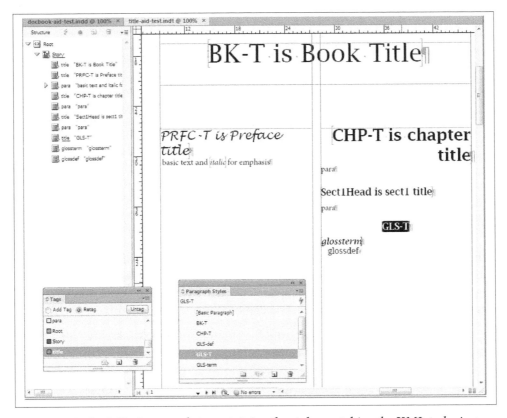

Figure 11-2. An InDesign template containing the styles matching the XML to be imported

Each of the example text paragraphs are tagged with either a `<title>` or `<para>` from the simple Tags menu. The "Map Tags to Styles" feature of InDesign is *not* used because there is not a 1:1 relationship between the tag names and style names. There are multiple styles that are based on the `<title>` tag. The Story Editor view of the InDesign template shows that each paragraph has been tagged and styled (Figure 11-3).

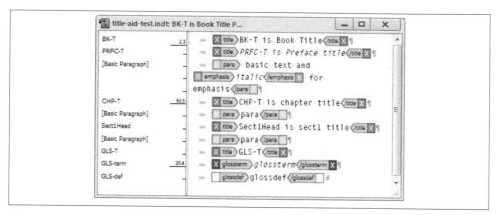

Figure 11-3. A simple XML template seen in Story Editor with tags viewable

If the InDesign template is exported as an IDML file, there is a list of all the styles inside the IDML; see "A Brief Note about IDML and ICML" (page 117). This style list can be used to get the name of every style the template designer has used so that a developer can extract the paragraph and character style names to create a style configuration file.

For example, by looking at the *Styles.xml* file (found in the IDML archive file for the sample InDesign template), the developer can find these style names:

```
<RootCharacterStyleGroup Self="u77">
    <CharacterStyle Self="CharacterStyle/$ID/[No character style]"
     Imported="false" Name="$ID/[No character style]" />
    <CharacterStyle Self="CharacterStyle/italic" Imported="false"
                    KeyboardShortcut="0 0" Name="italic"
                    FontStyle="Italic">
                    <!-- some code omitted for brevity -->
    </CharacterStyle>
</RootCharacterStyleGroup>
<RootParagraphStyleGroup Self="u76">
    <ParagraphStyle Self="ParagraphStyle/BK-T" Name="BK-T" Imported="false"
                    NextStyle="ParagraphStyle/BK-T" KeyboardShortcut="0 0"
                    PointSize="36" Hyphenation="false" SpaceBefore="72"
                    SpaceAfter="24" Justification="CenterAlign">
                    <!-- some code omitted for brevity -->
    </ParagraphStyle>
    <ParagraphStyle Self="ParagraphStyle/PRFC-T" Name="PRFC-T"
                    Imported="false"
                    NextStyle="ParagraphStyle/$ID/NormalParagraphStyle"
                    KeyboardShortcut="0 0" FontStyle="Italic"
                    PointSize="18" Hyphenation="false"
                    StartParagraph="NextColumn">
...
```

Using the list of styles from the IDML, and a sample of the layout to show how the styles are used, a developer can set up the appropriate values for each element.

After the XML with the `aid:` namespace attributes is imported, any matching style names will affect the appearance of the text when it is placed in the layout (Figure 11-4). Notice how the `<title>` element with the `aid:pstyle` `"GLS-T"` has been formatted as centered and bold, while the title of the preface is formatted as a script font.

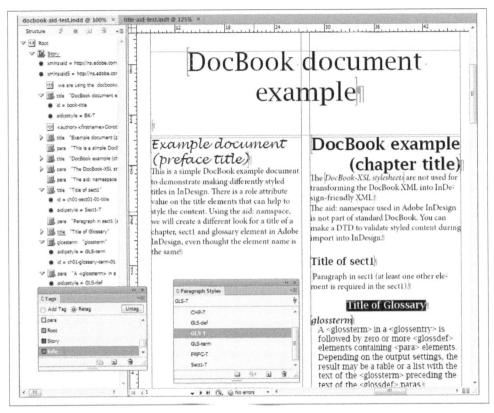

Figure 11-4. Content generated from DocBook with aid: namespace and id values that can be used to reconstruct DocBook XML

If there are multiple text flows to create from a single XML file, then the built-in `<Root>` element can have multiple child `<Story>` elements, each with its own `id`. Each story-level element can be dragged onto a different text flow in the layout.

As previously mentioned, the `id` values of all XML elements are particularly important to any kind of round-tripping that might occur. Style names alone won't provide enough data for the XSLT to reconstruct the original DocBook structure.

After the DocBook structure is re-established, you can use an XML comparison tool such as that built into Oxygen XML or another XML IDE to check the results.

This discussion just scratches the surface of what real round-tripping for DocBook, DITA, or other complex DTD may require. But the essential concepts here can provide the basis for a systematic downcast/upcast that will provide a good deal of a round-trip process.

 Developers should note that footnotes, cross-reference links, image metadata, and other common parts of complex XML DTDs are very difficult to create and manage in a round-trip scenario.

Brief Notes

A Brief Note about InCopy and XML

According to James Maidvald,

> InCopy can:
> Open an InDesign document to edit or add XML structure.
> Open an InDesign assignment or InCopy .INCX file to edit or add XML structure.
> Open an XML file directly.
> Create an XML file from scratch.

Maidvald's 2007 book is *Designer's Guide to Adobe InDesign and XML: Harness the Power of XML to Automate your Print and Web Workflows* (Adobe, 2007).

 Since version CS4, the *.icnx* file format has been replaced by the *.icml* file format, for interchanging InCopy files with CS4 and CS5. See "A Brief Note about IDML and ICML" (page 117).

InCopy files externalize InDesign text flows for copy editing without using InDesign. The licenses for InCopy are much cheaper than the ones for InDesign.

A designer assigns an InDesign text flow to an editor or writer as an assignment file. The writer or editor checks out and opens the assignment in InCopy, where the InDesign layout for the text flow can be seen, but not changed, by the person working on the text. Typically, the writer or editor can apply color swatches, make text bold, italic, bulleted, and so on, and apply approved paragraph and character styles.

It gets interesting when you want to create XML files but you don't want to have all the writers trying to make XML content in the same InDesign file. In this case, you can create XML files using a DTD in InCopy just as you would in InDesign. So each writer can create XML in their assigned text flow using the Story editor with tags viewable and switch to the other views to see how the text looks and whether it is overset for the assigned text flow. (There's also a view in InCopy that will show the exact word count and line breaks of the text flow.)

You can save InCopy files as *.icml* (the default format) or, if you have tagged them, you can save them as *.xml* files. Figure 12-1 shows XML tagged content in InCopy, styled with paragraph styles and exported as RTF, followed by its tagged content in XML (Example 12-1).

 Neither InDesign nor InCopy allow you to tag footnote content as XML elements. This seems to be a bug, not a feature, because when you export XML, it seems probable that you would want your footnote content exported, too. But your footnotes are nowhere to be found in the exported XML.

Tale of a Simple, Tagged Story

by inline byline, author_name element with style authorname

A paragraph of p element tagged text in the body of the story, which uses no DTD-defined XML, just *ad hoc* tags. All line breaks occur outside of the XML tag. This paragraph, of style p_first, is honored by its stylish drop cap.

Another paragraph tags along with a footnote.[9]

Footnotes can't be tagged in InDesign, and that's the end of the story.

---

[9] A footnote is a special object in InCopy and InDesign; because it is generated as a page component, there isn't a way to tag it directly in the InCopy or InDesign. So the footnote is not part of an XML export of an InCopy file.

However, when RTF exported from InCopy is imported into a Word document, the footnote comes along with the RTF content.

Figure 12-1. An InCopy file saved as RTF for import into Word

Example 12-1. XML content produced by saving an InCopy file as XML

```
<?xml version="1.0" encoding="UTF-8" standalone="yes"?>
<Story><title>A Tale of a Simple, Tagged Story</title> <byline>by <author_name>
inline byline,  author_name element with style authorname</author_name></byline>
<content> <p>A paragraph of p element tagged text in the body of the story, which
uses no DTD-defined XML, just <emphasis type="foreign_term">ad hoc</emphasis> tags.
All line breaks occur outside of the XML tag. This paragraph, of style p_first, is
honored by its stylish drop cap.</p> <p>Another paragraph tags along with a
footnote.<fnref></fnref></p> <p>Footnotes can&#8217;t be tagged in InDesign, and
that&#8217;s the end of the story.</p></content></Story>
```

Typically, each InCopy file is a Story element in the XML in the InDesign file, and all the Story elements are contained within the Root element in the XML Structure pane.

See the Adobe InDesign Help topics on InCopy, including "Work with stand-alone documents" and "Preparing XML files for K4 or InCopy workflows." Unfortunately, Adobe is not expansive with explanations about XML and InCopy; you may want to consult the SDK documentation.

 For managing InCopy XML files with version control, which some editorial and production workflows require, some content management solutions include InCopy file handling. Search online for "InCopy XML workflows."

A Brief Note about IDML and ICML

Adobe created new interchange document description formats for InDesign (IDML) and InCopy (ICML) for version CS4. Both of these formats are written in XML format. So technically, they are XML files. However, just as Microsoft did with Word when creating the *.docx* file format, Adobe has made the IDML (and ICML) file format a "package" of files in an archive format, which is not intuitive for finding what you want to know about XML content within an InDesign file. One of the best resources to start with is *Adobe InDesign Markup Language (IDML) Cookbook (http://www.adobe.com/ devnet/indesign/pdfs/idml-cookbook.pdf)*, which tells you which part of the package describes what XML-related features of the InDesign file. For example, in the XML section of the IDML Cookbook, you find the following:

Adjusting a Document's Structure

A document's structure is stored in the XML/BackingStory.xml file and within the story XML files that are marked up. The BackingStory contains top-level associations between content and structure. Text that is marked up within a story is in the individual story files. *Detailing this relationship is beyond the scope of this document.*[1] The Import XML Template sample demonstrates performing the equivalent of an XML import completely outside InDesign.

Notice that even Adobe thinks that this relationship between XML content and Stories (text flows) is hard to explain and "beyond the scope" of their own cookbook.

 An InCopy file is a single file, not a package, saved by default with the *.icml* extension. However, it can contain XML tagged content, just like an InDesign file.

To look at an IDML file with XML in it, take any InDesign file in CS4 or CS5 that you have tagged with some XML and export the file as IDML. To open the *.idml* archive file, use an archive-unpacking application such as WinZip, and you will see a set of folders and files as shown in Figure 12-2.

Figure 12-2. An IDML package file, showing the XML folder files

---

1. Emphasis added.

The contents of the files are interrelated. The *Tag.xml* file (Example 12-2) determines what is available in the Tags palette in InDesign and how each tag will be color-coded in InDesign.

Example 12-2. A sample Tags.xml file in an IDML package

```
<?xml version="1.0" encoding="UTF-8" standalone="yes"?>
<idPkg:Tags xmlns:idPkg="http://ns.adobe.com/AdobeInDesign/idml/1.0/packaging"
DOMVersion="7.0">
    <XMLTag Self="XMLTag/a" Name="a">
        <Properties>
            <TagColor type="enumeration">Green</TagColor>
        </Properties>
    </XMLTag>
    <XMLTag Self="XMLTag/b" Name="b">
        <Properties>
            <TagColor type="enumeration">Blue</TagColor>
        </Properties>
    </XMLTag>
    <XMLTag Self="XMLTag/c" Name="c">
        <Properties>
            <TagColor type="enumeration">Yellow</TagColor>
        </Properties>
    </XMLTag>
    </XMLTag>
</idPkg:Tags>
```

The BackingStory is a reference file to track which XML content is located in which Story (Example 12-3). It acts as a lookup only; despite its name, it does not contain any Story content.

Example 12-3. The cryptic BackingStory.xml file

```
<?xml version="1.0" encoding="UTF-8" standalone="yes"?>
<idPkg:BackingStory
xmlns:idPkg="http://ns.adobe.com/AdobeInDesign/idml/1.0/packaging" DOMVersion="7.0">
    <XmlStory Self="u5e" AppliedTOCStyle="n" TrackChanges="false" StoryTitle="$ID/"
    AppliedNamedGrid="n">
        <ParagraphStyleRange
          AppliedParagraphStyle="ParagraphStyle/[No paragraph style]">
            <CharacterStyleRange AppliedCharacterStyle="CharacterStyle/$ID/
            [No character style]">
                <XMLElement Self="di2" MarkupTag="XMLTag/Root">
                    <XMLElement Self="di2i3" MarkupTag="XMLTag/Story"
                      XMLContent="u733"/>
                    <XMLElement Self="di2i5" MarkupTag="XMLTag/Story"
                      XMLContent="u166e"/>
                    <XMLElement Self="di2i6" MarkupTag="XMLTag/Story"
                      XMLContent="u16fb"/>
                </XMLElement>
                <Content></Content>
```

```
        </CharacterStyleRange>
      </ParagraphStyleRange>
    </XmlStory>
</idPkg:BackingStory>
```

If you open the *u733.xml* file in the *Stories* folder, you will see that it starts off like this:

```
<?xml version="1.0" encoding="UTF-8" standalone="yes"?>
<idPkg:Story xmlns:idPkg="http://ns.adobe.com/AdobeInDesign/idml/1.0/packaging"
DOMVersion="7.0">
    <Story Self="u733" AppliedTOCStyle="n" TrackChanges="false"
      StoryTitle="$ID/" AppliedNamedGrid="n">
```

Somewhere further down in the *u733.xml* file, you will see an XML element with <Content> nested inside it:

```
<XMLElement Self="di2i3i1ib" MarkupTag="XMLTag/c" XMLContent="u733i15e2i8">
    <ParagraphStyleRange AppliedParagraphStyle="ParagraphStyle/tablecell">
        <CharacterStyleRange AppliedCharacterStyle="CharacterStyle/$ID/
          [No character style]">
            <Content>element c</Content>
        </CharacterStyleRange>
    </ParagraphStyleRange>
</XMLElement>
```

So you can see the relationship between *BackingStory.xml* (pointing to a Story file identified as "u733"), the *Tags.xml* file (defining a tag for an element <c>), and *u733.xml*, which uses the "c" tag in the MarkupTag attribute of the <XMLElement>.

When used with the InDesign Server and well-designed InDesign document templates, automating IDML provides a way to generate beautiful documents from XML content stored in a database or content management system. The Adobe specification and documentation for IDML runs to hundreds of pages. Most of the people who work with the IDML format of InDesign are XML experts.

No one in his right mind wants to read IDML code. But believe it or not, if you can generate exactly the required code in each type of file in the entire IDML package, and put the files in the correct folder structure, zip them and name them with an *.idml* extension, you too can create an entire InDesign file from code. You can create your own tags and tag your XML without even owning InDesign. I'll leave you with that thought.

Automating InDesign: The Power of IDML and ICML Programming

There are a number of developers and companies that have worked on solutions for making XML content in InDesign. Generally, every automation is expensive and time-consuming to work out, because every XML and InDesign publishing scenario involves different XML structure and different InDesign styles.

There are systems such as RSuite, Typefi, or K4 that may map DITA or DocBook to InDesign styles and layout objects through an interim DTD. These expensive systems provide for round-tripping the XML content as long as it is developed within their applications' specialized InDesign workflows.

There are InDesign developers who specialize in IDML or ICML programming. For example, they can make simultaneous ePubs with CSS related to the styles in InDesign and the complete laid-out InDesign files directly from source XML. Another example is creating complex ICML files for XML Shakespeare plays that include line numbering every fifth line and hyperlinks for cross-references, which is difficult to achieve in In-Design. Most of these types of conversions are one-way; they are not intended for round-tripping back from InDesign to XML.

An ICML developer's test case

Giuseppe Bonelli has provided an example file and instructions for making an ICML file from DocBook content. These instructions are included in the *readme* file for his example files, reproduced below:

The workflow for importing an XML file into a single InDesign text frame is very straightforward:

1. Prepare a *.indt* template containing the layout and the styles definitions.
2. Prepare the XSLT for transforming from the source DTD to ICML.
3. Apply the transform to the XML instance documents and save them as *[file name].icml*.
4. Open in InDesign a new document based on the template.
5. Use the file/place command to flow the *[filename].icml* file into the InDesign file.
6. Unlink the *[filename].icml* file from the links panel or open a new assignment to edit.
7. Copyfit, move figures, and tweak as necessary.
8. Save and export to PDF, HTML, or ePub.

The InDesign template can be prepared by a designer who does not know anything about XML and passed to an XML programmer who will implement the equivalent of *xml2icml.xslt* for the project.

You also can place the ICML file in a blank IDML document (i.e., without any style definition). The styles defined in the XSLT will be created upon import.

In principle, you can put the typography and the styles definition directly in the XSLT (just add the right attributes to the style definitions), but it usually is easier and cleaner to keep all the styling in the InDesign template and just define the style names in the XSLT (as has been done in this example).

The example files given here are very basic, but the XSLT is for the most part boilerplate code and can be easily modified. See the comments in the XSLT for details.

For complex layouts with more than one box, you cannot use ICML (unless you can have one XML for each box) and you must use a full IDML file. The basic principle is the same, but the XSLT programming is more complex. Usually this is best tackled by preparing an InDesign template with some filler text, export to IDML, look at the .idml files, and copy and paste the relevant XML structures/tags/attributes in the XSLT.

Note that whomever is going to import and edit the *.icml* file into InDesign does not need to know anything about XML.

The pragmatic approach outlined here can be used for incremental development of an XML to ICML or IDML process. Start small, see what results you get, redefine the requirements, iterate the code, and repeat.

Notice that this process is different from what is described in "The Challenge of Mapping Deep DTDs to Shallow InDesign Structures" (page 107) earlier in this book. In that process, XML structure is being created in the InDesign file. In this process, XML is converted to regular InDesign styled content, and nothing is generated in the XML Structure panel.

Let's look at the process in the example code in more detail. There are only a few styles defined in the InDesign template (Figure 12-3).

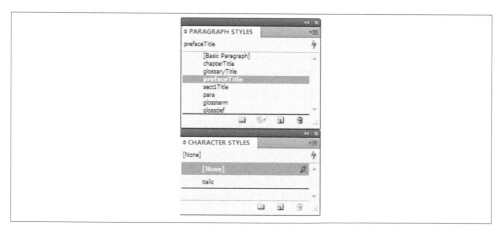

Figure 12-3. Styles in the InDesign template

The XML file is the same one that I used for the examples in the section Chapter 11:

```
<!DOCTYPE book>
<?xml-stylesheet type="text/xsl" href="docbook2ICML.xsl"?>
<book
 <bookinfo><title id="book-title"
  role="aid:pstyle='BK-T'">DocBook document example</title>
  <author></bookinfo>
 <preface>
  <title id="ch01-preface-title"  role="aid:pstyle='PRFC-T'">Example document
        (preface title)</title>
  <para>This is a simple DocBook example document to demonstrate making
        differently styled titles in InDesign. There is a role attribute value
        on the title elements that can help to style the content. Using the
        aid: namespace, we will create a different look for a title of a
        chapter, sect1, and glossary element in Adobe InDesign, even though
        the element name is the same.</para>
 </preface>
 <chapter>
  <title id="ch01-chapter-title"
  role="aid:pstyle='CHP-T'">DocBook example (chapter title)</title>
  <para>The <emphasis role="aid:cstyle='italic'">DocBook-XSL
        stylesheets</emphasis> are not used for transforming the DocBook XML
        into InDesign-friendly XML.</para>
  <para>The aid: namespace used in Adobe InDesign is not part of standard
        DocBook. You can make a DTD to validate styled content during import
        into InDesign.</para>
 ...
```

Here is an example of the XSLT template used to create the ICML XML (a story). Start by making a pair of variables for the version of InDesign and InCopy (also called a "snippet"). Notice that each character style of paragraph style in the InDesign template requires its own definition within the RootCharacterStyleGroup or the RootParagraphStyleGroup:

```
<!-- Fixed strings to indicate ID and ICML version and software version -->
    <!-- These are for my build of IDCS5.5 MacOSX -->
    <xsl:variable name="icml-decl-pi"><xsl:text>style="50" type="snippet"
     readerVersion="6.0" featureSet="257" product="7.5(142)"</xsl:text>
    </xsl:variable>
    <xsl:variable name="snippet-type-pi">
    <xsl:text>SnippetType="InCopyInterchange"</xsl:text></xsl:variable>
    <!-- ====================================================== -->
    <!-- Document styles, presets and document root -->
    <!-- ====================================================== -->
    <xsl:template match="book<!-- put here your source XML doc root tag
      name when making one text flow from the source file -->
        <xsl:processing-instruction name="aid"><xsl:value-of
          select="$icml-decl-pi"/>
         </xsl:processing-instruction>
        <xsl:processing-instruction name="aid">
         <xsl:value-of select="$snippet-type-pi"/></xsl:processing-instruction>
```

```
<Document DOMVersion="6.0" Self="docbook2Id-helloWorld">
    <RootCharacterStyleGroup Self="EAS_character_styles">
        <!-- define here the styles names you want in ID-->
        <!-- to see the full format options export to ICML from your
                ID template and use whatever option you need. Here we
                use the bare minimum needed-->
        <!-- you can define here all the typography, however, that is
                probably better done in the ID template -->
        <CharacterStyle Self="CharacterStyle/$ID/[No character style]"
            Name="$ID/[No character style]"/>
        <CharacterStyle Self="CharacterStyle/italic" Name="italic"/>
    </RootCharacterStyleGroup>
    <RootParagraphStyleGroup Self="EAS_paragraph_styles">
        <ParagraphStyle Self="ParagraphStyle/$ID/[No paragraph style]"
            Name="$ID/[No paragraph style]"/>
        <ParagraphStyle Self="ParagraphStyle/chapterTitle"
            Name="chapterTitle"/>
        <ParagraphStyle Self="ParagraphStyle/prefaceTitle"
            Name="prefaceTitle"/>
        <ParagraphStyle Self="ParagraphStyle/glossaryTitle"
            Name="glossaryTitle"/>
        <ParagraphStyle Self="ParagraphStyle/sect1Title"
            Name="sect1Title"/>
        <ParagraphStyle Self="ParagraphStyle/para"
            Name="para"/>
        <ParagraphStyle Self="ParagraphStyle/glossterm"
            Name="glossterm"/>
        <ParagraphStyle Self="ParagraphStyle/glossdef"
            Name="glossdef"/>
    </RootParagraphStyleGroup>
    <Story Self="default_story" AppliedTOCStyle="n"
        TrackChanges="false" StoryTitle="DefaultStory"
            AppliedNamedGrid="n">
        <StoryPreference OpticalMarginAlignment="false"
            OpticalMarginSize="12"
            FrameType="TextFrameType" StoryOrientation="Horizontal"
            StoryDirection="LeftToRightDirection"/>
        <InCopyExportOption IncludeGraphicProxies="true"
            IncludeAllResources="false"/>
        <xsl:apply-templates/>
    </Story>
</Document>
</xsl:template>
```

Once the styles are defined, you can process them in the Story element using `apply-templates`. The remainder of the XSLT example (Example 12-4) shows how to write an XSLT template to handle each XML element, how to use call-templates and pass a value, how to write one template to handle different types of `<title>` elements according to the parent element. There are also handlers to use the default paragraph $ID/[No para graph style] or character $ID/[No character style] styles if there is no specific style names to map them to in the InDesign template. The defaults make sure that all text shows up in InDesign and isn't dropped by accident.

Example 12-4. XSLT templates to process specific XML elements into paragraph and character styles

```
<!-- ========================================================= -->
<!-- Template definitions for transforming from docbook DTD to ICML -->
<!-- ========================================================= -->
<!-- Call template para-style-range passing style names as defined above
      and source content nodes to build ICML paras-->
<xsl:template match="bookinfo"/><!-- In this example we skip metadata.
 In a real case we will build a colophon -->
<xsl:template match="chapter">
    <xsl:apply-templates/>
</xsl:template>
<xsl:template match="preface">
    <xsl:call-template name="para-style-range">
        <xsl:with-param name="style-name">chapterLabel</xsl:with-param>
        <xsl:with-param name="textStr" select="'Preface'"/>
    </xsl:call-template>
    <xsl:apply-templates/>
</xsl:template>
<xsl:template match="glossary">
    <xsl:call-template name="para-style-range">
        <xsl:with-param name="style-name">chapterLabel</xsl:with-param>
        <xsl:with-param name="textStr" select="'Glossary'"/>
    </xsl:call-template>
    <xsl:apply-templates/>
</xsl:template>
<!-- make titles use different styles according to their parent DJH Nov.2012 -->
<xsl:template match="title[parent::chapter] | title[parent::glossary] |
                    title[parent::preface] | title[parent::sect1]">
    <xsl:variable name="myParent">
     <xsl:value-of select="name(..)"/><xsl:text>Title</xsl:text></xsl:variable>
    <xsl:call-template name="para-style-range">
        <xsl:with-param name="style-name"><xsl:value-of select="$myParent"/>
          </xsl:with-param>
        <xsl:with-param name="ContentNodes" select="node()"/>
    </xsl:call-template>
</xsl:template
<xsl:template match="glossentry">
    <xsl:apply-templates/>
</xsl:template>
<xsl:template match="glossterm">
    <xsl:call-template name="para-style-range">
        <xsl:with-param name="style-name">glossterm</xsl:with-param>
        <xsl:with-param name="ContentNodes" select="node()"/>
    </xsl:call-template>
</xsl:template>
```

```
<xsl:template match="glossdef">
    <xsl:call-template name="para-style-range">
        <xsl:with-param name="style-name">glossdef</xsl:with-param>
        <xsl:with-param name="ContentNodes" select="para"/>
    </xsl:call-template>
</xsl:template>

<!-- this is the default para. Specialize it as needed using source xml
     semantics/structure or explicit styles in attributes and or roles -->
<xsl:template match="para">
    <xsl:call-template name="para-style-range">
        <xsl:with-param name="style-name">para</xsl:with-param>
        <xsl:with-param name="ContentNodes" select="node()"/>
    </xsl:call-template>
</xsl:template>

<!-- ========================================================== -->
<!-- Inlines -->
<!-- ========================================================== -->
<xsl:template match="emphasis[contains(@role, 'italic')]"
    mode="character-style-range">
    <xsl:call-template name="char-style-range">
        <xsl:with-param name="style-name">italic</xsl:with-param>
    </xsl:call-template>
</xsl:template>
<xsl:template match="text()" mode="character-style-range">
    <xsl:call-template name="char-style-range"/>
</xsl:template>

<!-- ========================================================== -->
<!-- Named templates called to build ID para and char ranges -->
<!-- (Probably no changes needed below -->
<!-- ========================================================== -->
<xsl:template name="para-style-range">
    <!-- The name of the paragraph style in InDesign -->
    <xsl:param name="style-name">$ID/[No paragraph style]</xsl:param>
    <xsl:param name="ContentNodes"/>
    <xsl:param name="textStr" select="''"/>
     <!-- use this for inserting fixed strings (e.g. chapter labels) -->
    <ParagraphStyleRange>
        <xsl:attribute name="AppliedParagraphStyle">
            <xsl:value-of select="concat('ParagraphStyle/', $style-name)"/>
        </xsl:attribute>
        <xsl:choose>
            <xsl:when test="$ContentNodes">
                <xsl:apply-templates select="$ContentNodes"
                    mode="character-style-range"/>
            </xsl:when>
            <xsl:when test="$textStr != ''">
                <CharacterStyleRange>
                    <xsl:attribute name="AppliedCharacterStyle">
                        $ID/[No character style]</xsl:attribute>
```

```
            <Content><xsl:value-of select="$textStr"/></Content>
        </CharacterStyleRange>
    </xsl:when>
    </xsl:choose>
    <Br/>
    </ParagraphStyleRange>
</xsl:template>

<xsl:template name="char-style-range">
    <!-- The name of the character style in InDesign -->
    <xsl:param name="style-name">$ID/[No character style]</xsl:param>
    <CharacterStyleRange>
        <xsl:attribute name="AppliedCharacterStyle">
            <xsl:value-of select="concat('CharacterStyle/', $style-name)"/>
        </xsl:attribute>
        <Content><xsl:value-of select="."/></Content>
    </CharacterStyleRange>
</xsl:template>
```

The resulting ICML file includes the text of the DocBook XML elements wrapped in the ICML XML elements, ready to import into the InDesign file.

ICML is verbose, so here is just a small example of the output, where you can see that in a single paragraph, the character style switches between the default and the named character style "italic":

```
<ParagraphStyleRange AppliedParagraphStyle="ParagraphStyle/para">
<CharacterStyleRange AppliedCharacterStyle="CharacterStyle/$ID/
    [No character style]"><Content>The </Content></CharacterStyleRange>
<CharacterStyleRange AppliedCharacterStyle="CharacterStyle/italic">
    <Content>DocBook-XSL stylesheets</Content></CharacterStyleRange>
<CharacterStyleRange AppliedCharacterStyle=
    "CharacterStyle/$ID/[No character style]">
<Content> are not used for transforming the DocBook XML into InDesign-friendly
XML.</Content></CharacterStyleRange><Br/></ParagraphStyleRange>
```

You can see the italic words in Figure 12-4.

The results are nice and clean: formatted text in the InDesign file after the ICML is placed. Notice that there are no Tag names except the default Root, and no structure except the Root in the Structure panel. So this technique is *not* intended for XML round-tripping. It is possible to add support for the XML structure and write the structure in IDML but doing so requires a lot of IDML knowledge.

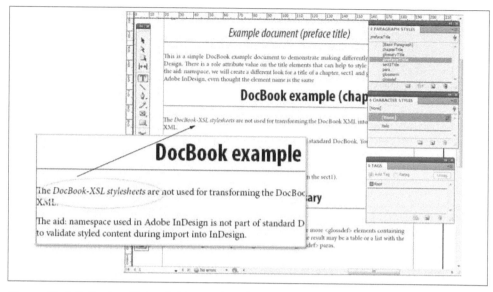

Figure 12-4. InDesign file with ICML placed in it

Summary

I think that Adobe has given the world some serious tools to work with, and I hope that they will decide to keep improving the XML features of their products.

If you work with InDesign as a layout tool, you'll find that there are lots of ways to add value to your skills by using XML. It's a bit esoteric for most layout people, but if you try a few things, XML tends to get your interest.

You can combine XML content with non-XML content in a single document (and I'm not talking about just headers and footers and boilerplate text). You can have multiple Story elements in a Root element and flow from text frame to text frame, threading frames to jump from page to page as desired. You can use the list numbering and other automatic formatting in InDesign on XML content. And it's easy to style XML content with colors, fonts, and even skew effects in InDesign (Figure 12-5)—"stylish structure," indeed.

Even more enticing is the ability to use a different set of styles and layout to completely change how XML content looks solely by making new InDesign templates with new style definitions. The InDesign template provides the "skin" for the content, so any XML that maps to the styles can be changed to a different look by using a different InDesign template.

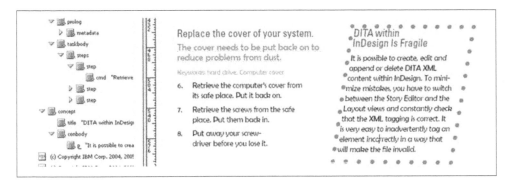

Figure 12-5. XML content can look like any other InDesign content, including auto-numbered lists and skewed text boxes (structure at left, presentation at right)

If you are an XML-whacker already, but you haven't ever used it in a desktop publishing application, I hope that Chapter 10 has gotten you interested. You are sure to try something that I haven't covered here, so consider letting us know by sending us your comments to improve this book.

If you want to see Adobe continue to enhance the XML capabilities for do-it-yourselfers (not just for people who can afford high-end server-based Adobe apps), then send them suggestions and show off what you do with XML and InDesign. Personally, I'm planning to try a lot more types of layouts and XSLT with InDesign—and maybe try my hand at scripting more XML, too.

Resources

The InDesign forum at Adobe's site (*http://www.adobe.com/support/forums/*) is a good place to find examples, pose questions, and get help on any XML import, tagging, or export topic.

InDesign Resources

Real World Adobe InDesign CS6 and previous editions for other versions, by Olav Martin Kvern, David Blatner, and Bob Bringhurst (Peachpit, 2012)

Adobe InDesign Markup Language (IDML) Cookbook, online resource (free PDF download)

Scripting InDesign with JavaScript, by Peter Kahrel (O'Reilly, 2010)

- Updated August 2010. Peter Kahrel updated this Short Cut to cover InDesign CS5. He says: "In Adobe InDesign CS6, the changes to InDesign's scripting DOM are absolutely minimal. Therefore, the information in this title is valid and up to date for CS6."

InDesign CS5 Automation Using XML & JavaScript, by Grant Gamble (CreateSpace, 2011)

AppleScripting Adobe InDesign CS5 and CS5.5, by Shirley W. Hopkins (CreateSpace, 2011)

XML Resources

Adobe InDesign CS3 and XML: A Technical Reference (http://adobe.ly/13egAhi), free PDF (an older reference, but it contains a lot of useful content)

There are many excellent general XML references online, ranging from books by O'Reilly Media authors to W3C specifications to code samples for developers. I recommend:

XML in a Nutshell, 3rd ed., by Elliotte Rusty Harold and W. Scott Means (O'Reilly, 2004)

XML in Easy Steps, 2nd ed. by Mike McGrath (In Easy Steps Ltd., 2007)

XSLT Resources

XSLT Cookbook, 2nd ed., by Sal Mangano (O'Reilly Media, 2005). *My favorite XSLT book.*

XSLT for Dummies (http://shop.oreilly.com/product/9780764536519.do), by Richard Wagner (O'Reilly, 2011)

XSLT, 2nd Edition (*http://shop.oreilly.com/product/9780764536519.do*), by Doug Tidwell (O'Reilly, 2008)

About the Author

Dorothy Hoskins is an XML evangelist, always learning new things to help her play with XML (like podcasting and AJAXian web development), but her true love is the development of processes that tie together various applications for publishing XML to both print and web.

From her initial career as a graphic artist and designer/illustrator, she has been led far afield by her interests in holography, interactive multimedia, and all things XML. Besides creating server-side XSLT for a global corporation's website, she has created publishing workflows for importing database-derived XML into Adobe's FrameMaker and InDesign CS2 products. She has presented numerous times on XML and XSL for the Society for Technical Communication and SUNY/Higher Ed groups.

She resides with her family in western New York, where she finds the weather a refreshing change from her native Florida.

Colophon

The animal on the cover of *XML and InDesign* is the blue swimmer crab (*Portunus pelagicus*).

The cover image is from Johnson's Natural History. The cover font is Adobe ITC Garamond. The text font is Adobe Minion Pro; the heading font is Adobe Myriad Condensed; and the code font is Dalton Maag's Ubuntu Mono.

Have it your way.

Get even more for your money.

Join the O'Reilly Community, and register the O'Reilly books you own. It's free, and you'll get:

- $4.99 ebook upgrade offer
- 40% upgrade offer on O'Reilly print books
- Membership discounts on books and events
- Free lifetime updates to ebooks and videos
- Multiple ebook formats, DRM FREE
- Participation in the O'Reilly community
- Newsletters
- Account management
- 100% Satisfaction Guarantee

Signing up is easy:

1. **Go to: oreilly.com/go/register**
2. **Create an O'Reilly login.**
3. **Provide your address.**
4. **Register your books.**

Note: English-language books only

To order books online:
oreilly.com/store

For questions about products or an order:
orders@oreilly.com

To sign up to get topic-specific email announcements and/or news about upcoming books, conferences, special offers, and new technologies:
elists@oreilly.com

For technical questions about book content:
booktech@oreilly.com

To submit new book proposals to our editors:
proposals@oreilly.com

O'Reilly books are available in multiple DRM-free ebook formats. For more information:
oreilly.com/ebooks

Spreading the knowledge of innovators   oreilly.com

Milton Keynes UK
Ingram Content Group UK Ltd.
UKHW050031060324
438908UK00010B/1351